I0412198

June 2014

CONFLICT MINERALS

Stakeholder Options for Responsible Sourcing Are Expanding, but More Information on Smelters Is Needed

GAO-14-575

CONFLICT MINERALS

Stakeholder Options for Responsible Sourcing Are Expanding, but More Information on Smelters Is Needed

GAO Highlights

Highlights of GAO-14-575, a report to congressional committees

Why GAO Did This Study

Armed groups in eastern DRC continue to commit severe human rights abuses and profit from the exploitation of minerals, according to reports from the United Nations. Congress included a provision in the 2010 Dodd-Frank Wall Street Reform and Consumer Protection Act to address the trade in "conflict minerals"—tin, tantalum, tungsten, and gold. Section 1502 of the Act directed several U.S. agencies to report or focus on issues related to conflict minerals.

This report examines, among other things, (1) the extent to which relevant U.S. agencies have undertaken activities related to responsible sourcing of conflict minerals and (2) what is known about the status of, and information provided by, stakeholder initiatives focused on responsible sourcing of conflict minerals from the DRC and adjoining countries. GAO reviewed and analyzed documents and data covering 2003 through 2014. We interviewed representatives from State, USAID, SEC, Commerce, nongovernmental organizations, industry, and international organizations who are cognizant of conflict minerals issues.

What GAO Recommends

GAO recommends that the Secretary of Commerce provide Congress a plan that outlines the steps, with associated timeframes, to develop and report the required information about smelters and refiners of conflict minerals worldwide. Commerce concurred with GAO's recommendation and noted that it will submit a listing of all known conflict minerals processing facilities worldwide to Congress by September 1, 2014.

View GAO-14-575. For more information, contact Kimberly M. Gianopoulos at (202) 512-8612 or gianopoulosk@gao.gov.

What GAO Found

Since the Dodd-Frank Wall Street Reform and Consumer Protection Act (the Act) was passed in 2010, relevant U.S. agencies have undertaken various activities related to responsible sourcing of conflict minerals from the Democratic Republic of the Congo (DRC) and adjoining countries. In response to the Act, the Department of State (State) and the U.S. Agency for International Development (USAID) developed a strategy in 2011 to address the linkages among human rights abuses, armed groups, and the mining of conflict minerals and are implementing various strategy objectives. The Securities and Exchange Commission (SEC) issued a rule in 2012 requiring certain companies to disclose the source and chain of custody of necessary conflict minerals in their products. However, the Department of Commerce (Commerce) has not yet compiled a list of all conflict minerals processing facilities—smelters and refiners—known worldwide, required by January 2013 by the Act. Commerce cited difficulties with, for example, tracking conflict minerals operations but told GAO that it had completed outreach efforts with the majority of stakeholders. Commerce did not have a plan of action, with associated time frames, for developing and reporting on the list of conflict minerals processing facilities worldwide. Standard practices in program and project management include, among other things, developing a plan to execute specific projects needed to obtain defined results within a specific time frame. An action plan with timeframes could better position Commerce to report on the status of its efforts to produce a final list to Congress and to hold its personnel accountable for completing activities.

Over the past several years, a number of stakeholders—foreign governments, multilateral organizations, and industry associations, among others—have expanded, or made plans to expand, initiatives focused on responsible sourcing of conflict minerals in the DRC and adjoining countries. These stakeholder initiatives, such as in-region tracing of conflict minerals and development of guidance documents and audit protocols, have grown to include new mine sites, countries, and smelters. For example, the Conflict-Free Smelter Program, an industry-led effort, has expanded from 26 smelters certified as conflict-free in 2013 to 85 smelters as of April 25, 2014 (see table). New stakeholder initiatives are also underway or planned in the region, including the first responsible sourcing initiative in the Congo-Brazzaville. Some initiatives have yielded publicly available information, including data on production of conflict-free minerals and export data. For example, one stakeholder has reported production data for tin, tungsten, and tantalum from three provinces in the DRC and in Rwanda.

Number of Smelters and Refiners in the Conflict-Free Smelter Program as of April 25, 2014

Mineral	Number of smelters/refiners certified as compliant	Number of smelters/refiners working toward certification	Total
Tantalum	28	1	29
Tin	13	14	27
Tungsten	1	8	9
Gold	43	2	45
Total	85	25	110

Source: Conflict-Free Sourcing Initiative data, GAO (analysis).

United States Government Accountability Office

Contents

Tables

Figures

Abbreviations

BGR	German Federal Institute for Geosciences and Natural Resources
CFSI	Conflict-Free Sourcing Initiative
CFTI	Conflict-Free Tin Initiative
Commerce	United States Department of Commerce
DHS	Demographic and Health Survey
Dodd-Frank Act	Dodd-Frank Wall Street Reform and Consumer Protection Act
DRC	Democratic Republic of the Congo
EICC	Electronic Industry Citizenship Coalition
GeSI	Global e-Sustainability Initiative
EU	European Union
ICGLR	International Conference on the Great Lakes Region
iTSCi	ITRI Tin Supply Chain Initiative
LBMA	London Bullion Market Association
M-23	March 23 Movement
MONUSCO	UN Organization Stabilization Mission in the Democratic Republic of the Congo
NGO	nongovernmental organization
OECD	Organisation for Economic Co-operation and Development
PPA	Public-Private Alliance for Responsible Minerals Trade
SEC	Securities and Exchange Commission
State	United States Department of State
UN	United Nations
USAID	United States Agency for International Development

GAO
U.S. GOVERNMENT ACCOUNTABILITY OFFICE

441 G St. N.W.
Washington, DC 20548

June 26, 2014

Congressional Committees

Over the past decade, the United States and the international community have sought to improve security in the Democratic Republic of the Congo (DRC), the site of one of the world's worst humanitarian crises. The International Rescue Committee has previously estimated that since 1998, more than 5.4 million people have died in the DRC as a result of this crisis, which has also destabilized the minerals-rich eastern part of the country, created insecurity, displaced thousands of people, and perpetuated a cycle of poverty. As we previously reported, illegal armed groups and some units of the Congolese national military have committed severe human rights abuses and mass killings and profited from the illegal exploitation of minerals originating in eastern DRC, particularly in the provinces of North Kivu and South Kivu.[1] Despite some success in efforts to improve security in eastern DRC—notably, the November 2013 defeat of M-23, an illegal armed group,[2] as well as campaigns against other illegal armed groups—the UN reported that as of December 2013, illegal armed groups in eastern DRC continued to pose a threat to security, to be responsible for human rights abuses and displacements of people, and to derive funding from the illicit production, trade, and smuggling of conflict minerals.[3]

Citing the continuing urgency of the humanitarian situation and the need to take action, in July 2010, Congress included in the Dodd-Frank Wall Street Reform and Consumer Protection Act (hereafter referred to as the

---

[1] GAO, *The Democratic Republic of the Congo: U.S. Agencies Should Take Further Actions to Contribute to the Effective Regulation and Control of the Minerals Trade in Eastern Democratic Republic of the Congo*, GAO-10-1030 (Washington, D.C.: Sept. 30, 2010).

[2] M-23 was created in May 2012 in eastern DRC and surrendered to DRC forces in November 2013.

[3] United Nations Security Council, "Letter dated 12 December 2013 from the Group of Experts on the Democratic Republic of the Congo addressed to the Chair of the Security Council Committee established pursuant to resolution 1533 (2004) concerning the Democratic Republic of the Congo," Annex to "Letter dated 22 January 2014 from the Coordinator of the Group of Experts on the Democratic Republic of the Congo addressed to the President of the Security Council," S/2014/42 (Jan. 23, 2014).

Act or Dodd-Frank Act) provisions pertaining to trade involving conflict minerals—tantalum, tin, tungsten, and gold.[4] Section 1502 of the Act directed several U.S. agencies—the Securities and Exchange Commission (SEC), the Department of State (State), the U.S. Agency for International Development (USAID), and the Department of Commerce (Commerce)—to take certain actions to implement the Act's conflict minerals provisions, including provisions related to responsible sourcing of conflict minerals from the DRC and the adjoining countries.[5] The Act specifically directed the SEC to promulgate a rule, which SEC issued in August 2012, that requires certain issuers to disclose annually to SEC whether any of such minerals are necessary to the functionality or production of products manufactured, or contracted to be manufactured, by the issuer originated in the DRC or adjoining country and if so, to provide an additional report.[6] The Act also mandated GAO to report, beginning in 2012 and annually thereafter, on the effectiveness of the SEC rule in promoting peace and security in the DRC and adjoining countries, and annually, beginning in 2011, on the rate of sexual violence in war-torn areas of DRC and adjoining countries, among other things.

To address our mandates, since July 2011 we have issued several reports on topics ranging from the rate of sexual violence in the DRC and adjoining countries to SEC's rule and initiatives focused on responsible

---

[4]The Dodd-Frank Act defines conflict minerals as columbite-tantalite (coltan), cassiterite, gold, wolframite, or their derivatives, or any other mineral or its derivatives that are determined by the Secretary of State to be financing conflict in the DRC or an adjoining country. See Pub. L. No. 111-203 §1502, (e)(4). Columbite-tantalite (coltan), cassiterite, and wolframite are the ores from which tantalum, tin, and tungsten, respectively, are processed.

[5]In this report, the countries adjoining DRC—Angola, Burundi, Central African Republic, the Republic of the Congo, Rwanda, South Sudan, Tanzania, Uganda, and Zambia—are often termed "Dodd-Frank affected countries."

[6]Under the rule, SEC-reporting companies with "necessary" conflict minerals in products they manufactured or contracted to have manufactured must conduct a "reasonable country of origin inquiry" to determine whether their conflict minerals originated in the DRC or adjoining countries. If none of their conflict minerals originated in that region, they must file a Form SD to disclose the reasonable country of origin inquiry they conducted and the results. If any of a company's "necessary" conflict minerals originated in the DRC or adjoining countries, the company must exercise due diligence on the source and chain of custody of its conflict minerals and also file a Conflict Minerals Report.

sourcing of minerals.[7] Because the first SEC-required disclosures of manufacturers' use of conflict minerals were not due to SEC until June 2014, and because sufficient time must elapse to allow the rule's full impact to materialize, we have not yet addressed the effectiveness of SEC's conflict minerals rule as required under the legislation. Moreover, our ability to report on the rule's effectiveness will depend on the availability of information on stakeholder initiatives to, for example, monitor, ensure, or report on responsible sourcing of conflict minerals from the DRC and adjoining countries.[8] Consequently, in this report, we examine

1. the extent to which relevant U.S. agencies have taken actions related to the responsible sourcing of conflict minerals;

2. what is known about the status of, and any information provided by, stakeholder initiatives focused on responsible sourcing of conflict minerals from the DRC and adjoining countries; and

3. any new information about the rate of sexual violence in eastern DRC and three adjoining countries—Burundi, Rwanda, and Uganda—that has become available since we issued our 2013 report.[9]

To address our first and second objectives, we reviewed and analyzed available data covering 2003 through 2014 on conflict minerals from the DRC and adjoining countries and from responsible sourcing initiatives, as well as reports and other documents from relevant U.S. agencies, foreign governments, multilateral organizations, nongovernmental organizations (NGOs), and industry associations. Because the data were not used to

---

[7]GAO, *The Democratic Republic of the Congo: Information on the Rate of Sexual Violence in War-Torn Eastern DRC and Adjoining Countries*, GAO-11-702 (Washington, D.C.: July 13, 2011); *Conflict Minerals Disclosure Rule: SEC's Actions and Stakeholder-Developed Initiatives*, GAO-12-763 (Washington, D.C.: July 16, 2012); *SEC Conflict Minerals Rule: Information on Responsible Sourcing and Companies Affected*, GAO-13-689 (Washington, D.C.: July 18, 2013). In our 2012 report, we addressed, for example, a congressional mandate that asked us to describe any issues that the SEC encountered in promulgating a conflict minerals disclosure rule. In our 2013 report, we addressed, for example, a mandate that asked us to describe information that may be publicly available about entities that use conflict minerals but are not required to report to SEC under the rule.

[8]Stakeholders include relevant U.S. agencies; foreign governments; multilateral organizations, such as the Organization for Economic Cooperation and Development (OECD); nongovernmental organizations (NGOs); and industry associations.

[9]GAO-13-689.

support findings, conclusions, or recommendations, we did not assess their reliability. We also interviewed State, USAID, Commerce, and SEC officials as well as stakeholder representatives from international organizations, NGOs, and industry associations who are cognizant of conflict minerals issues. We selected these stakeholders based on their expertise on responsible sourcing issues, because they represented a range of perspectives on conflict minerals, and because we had established contacts with these entities on our last review.[10] In addition, some of the stakeholders we talked to have been working on the ground in the DRC. The stakeholders we spoke with constitute a nongeneralizable sample, and the information we gathered from them cannot be used to infer views of other stakeholders cognizant of conflict minerals issues. To address our third objective, we reviewed and analyzed relevant documents and interviewed representatives from State, USAID, various UN agencies, relevant NGOs, and researchers to identify any new data on sexual violence. Specifically, we followed up with officials from those groups we interviewed for our prior review on sexual violence rates in eastern DRC and adjoining countries.[11] We also conducted Internet literature searches to identify new academic articles containing any additional information available since our 2013 report. See appendix I for a complete description of our scope and methodology.

We conducted this performance audit from September 2013 to June 2014 in accordance with generally accepted government auditing standards. Those standards require that we plan and perform the audit to obtain sufficient, appropriate evidence to provide a reasonable basis for our findings and conclusions based on our audit objectives. We believe that the evidence obtained provides a reasonable basis for our findings and conclusions based on our audit objectives.

---

[10]GAO-13-689.

[11]GAO-13-689.

Background

Brief History of Conflict in the DRC and the Region

The DRC is a vast, mineral-rich nation with an estimated population of about 75 million people and an area that is roughly one-quarter the size of the United States, according to the UN. The map in figure 1 shows the DRC's provinces and adjoining countries.

Figure 1: Map of the Democratic Republic of the Congo with Provinces and Adjoining Countries

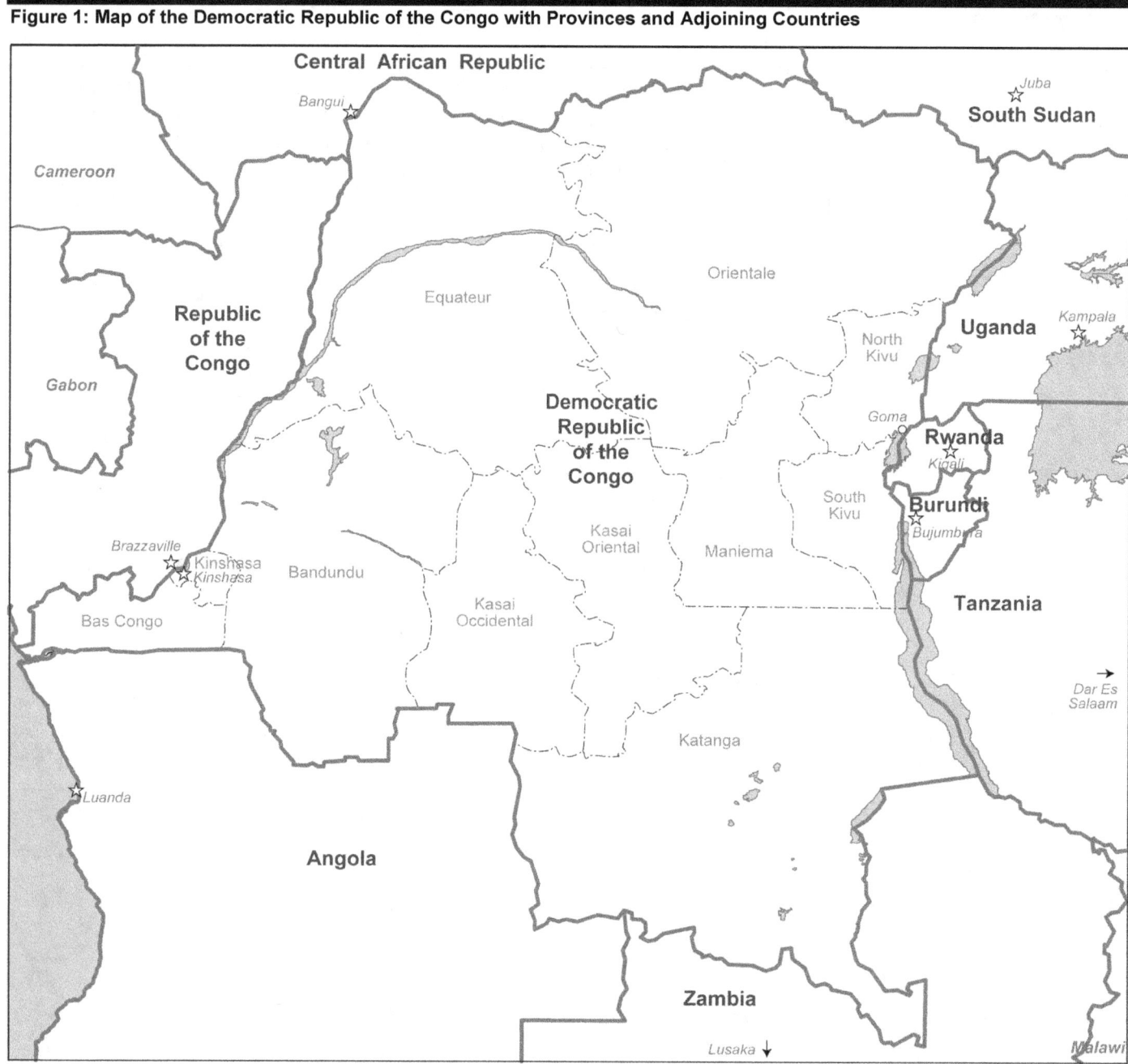

Source: GAO based on UN map. | GAO-14-575

Since its independence in 1960, the DRC has undergone political upheaval, including a civil war, according to State. In particular, the eastern DRC has continued to be plagued by violence often perpetrated by illegal armed groups and some members of the Congolese national military against civilians. In November 2012, M-23, an illegal armed group, occupied the city of Goma and other cities in eastern DRC and clashed with the Congolese national army. During this time, the UN reported numerous cases of sexual violence against civilians, including women and children, that were perpetrated by armed groups and some members of the Congolese national military.[12] Although M-23 eventually withdrew from the cities, the group's presence in the region continued. In December 2012, the Ugandan president began to broker peace talks, known as the Kampala Dialogue, between M-23 and the DRC government, aimed at reaching a final and principled agreement that ensured the disarmament and demobilization of M-23 and accountability for human rights abuses. The M-23 was defeated in November 2013 by the Congolese national military with support from UN forces. In December 2013, the former M-23 and the DRC each signed individual declarations that, among other things, set out the conditions for the disarmament, demobilization, and reintegration of M23 into Congolese society and called for those responsible for war crimes and crimes against humanity to be held accountable.

Prior to the defeat of M-23, in February 2013, the 11 countries in the region adopted the "Peace, Security and Cooperation Framework for the Democratic Republic of the Congo and the Region."[13] Some of the

---

[12]The Office of the High Commissioner for Human Rights and the United Nations Organization Stabilization Mission in the Democratic Republic of the Congo (MONUSCO) issued a report in May 2013 on mass rapes and other violations of human rights committed in Minova, a town in South Kivu, and surrounding areas in November 2012. The report documented 135 cases of sexual violence perpetrated by elements of the Congolese national army in and around the town of Minova as units retreated from the front lines.

[13]The eleven signatories to the framework were Angola, Burundi, the Central Africa Republic, the DRC, the Republic of the Congo (also known Congo-Brazzaville), Rwanda, South Africa, South Sudan, Tanzania, Uganda, and Zambia. The UN Secretary-General, the Chairperson of the African Union Commission, the Chairperson of the Southern African Development Community, and the Chairperson of the International Conference on the Great Lakes Region signed the agreement as witnesses. In January 2014, two additional countries, Kenya and Sudan, also signed the framework. According to the UN, the framework encompasses commitments at the national, regional and international levels to bring peace and stability to the eastern DRC and the region.

GAO-14-575 Conflict Minerals

adjoining countries in the region have also experienced recent turmoil, which has led to flows of large numbers of refugees into the DRC in addition to internally displaced persons.[14] The United Nations High Commissioner for Refugees (UNHCR) estimated, as of mid 2013, that there were close to 50,000 refugees from the Central African Republic, in addition to over 120,000 refugees from other countries, as well as around 2.6 million internally displaced persons living in camps or with host families in the DRC.

U.S. Government Response to Conflict in the DRC

Congress has focused on issues related to the DRC for almost a decade. In 2006, Congress passed the Democratic Republic of Congo Relief, Security, and Democracy Promotion Act of 2006,[15] stating that U.S policy is to engage with governments working for peace and security throughout the DRC and hold accountable individuals, entities, and countries working to destabilize the government. In July 2010, Congress passed the Dodd-Frank Act, which included several provisions in section 1502 of the Act concerning conflict minerals in the DRC and adjoining countries. The Act directs State, USAID, SEC, and Commerce to take steps on matters related to the implementation of those provisions (see text box).

Provisions in the Dodd-Frank Act Related to Conflict Minerals in the DRC and Adjoining Countries

- Section 1502(a) states that "it is the sense of the Congress that the exploitation and trade of conflict minerals originating in the Democratic Republic of the Congo is helping to finance conflict characterized by extreme levels of violence in the eastern Democratic Republic of the Congo, particularly sexual- and gender-based violence, and contributing to an emergency humanitarian situation therein, warranting the provisions of section 13(p) of the Securities Exchange Act of 1934, as added by subsection (b)."

- Section 1502(b) requires SEC, in consultation with State, to promulgate disclosure and reporting regulations regarding the use of conflict minerals from DRC and adjoining countries.

- Section 1502(c) requires State and USAID to develop, among other things, a strategy to address the linkages among human rights abuses, armed groups, the mining of conflict minerals, and commercial products.

- Section 1502(d) requires that Commerce report, among other things, a listing of all known conflict minerals processing facilities worldwide.

Source: GAO analysis. | GAO-14-575

---

[14]According to the UN, internally displaced persons are people who have not crossed an international border but have moved to a different region than the one they call home within their own country to escape war, persecution, or terror.

[15]Pub. L. No. 109-456.

In addition, in July 2013, the United States appointed the current Special Envoy for the Great Lakes Region and the DRC, whose office develops and leads the implementation of U.S. regional policy on cross-border security, political, economic and social issues. The Special Envoy leads U.S. efforts to support the implementation of the Peace, Security, and Cooperation Framework Agreement, including the development and implementation of a comprehensive strategy to stop human suffering and violence in the region, by promoting political, economic, and social reconciliation.

International Response to Conflict in the DRC

In 1999, the UN Security Council authorized peacekeeping operations in the DRC, known as the UN Organization Mission in Democratic Republic of the Congo (MONUC).[16] MONUC's mission included achieving a ceasefire and protecting civilians and other nonmilitary personnel from threats of physical violence. In 2010, MONUC was replaced by the UN Organization Stabilization Mission in the Democratic Republic of the Congo (MONUSCO), whose priorities also include protecting civilians and stabilizing the country.

The international community has also responded to the conflict in the DRC and adjoining countries by appointing special envoys to the region. For example, in March 2013, the UN appointed a Special Envoy of the Secretary-General for the Great Lakes Region to support the implementation of the 11-nation Peace, Security and Cooperation Framework for the Democratic Republic of the Congo and the Region.[17] In June 2013, the UN also appointed the current Special Representative of the Secretary-General for the Democratic Republic of the Congo and Head of MONUSCO. Both the European Union and African Union also have appointed representatives for the Great Lakes Region. To address imminent threats to peace and security, the UN Security Council also authorized the deployment of a force intervention brigade within the current peacekeeping operations in the DRC on March 28, 2013. The

[16]Initially, MONUC's focus was on the ceasefire and disengagement of forces and maintenance of liaison with all parties involved with the civil war, but the operation expanded to include the effective protection of civilians, humanitarian personnel, and human rights defenders under imminent threat of physical violence.

[17]According to the UN, the envoy's key tasks include undertaking good offices to strengthen the relations between the signatories of the framework, revitalizing existing accords and coordinating the international engagement.

GAO-14-575 Conflict Minerals

objectives of the new force based in North Kivu province are to neutralize armed groups, reduce the threat they pose to state authority and civilian security, and make space for stabilization activities.[18]

In addition, the European Union (EU) is exploring possible legislation related to conflict minerals and responsible sourcing.[19] According to a European Commission release, in March 2014, the EU proposed a draft regulation setting up an EU system of self-certification for importers of tin, tantalum, tungsten, and gold for imports into the EU. The draft regulation indicated that the self-certification would align with the Organization for Economic Cooperation and Development's (OECD) "OECD Due Diligence Guidance for Responsible Supply Chains of Minerals from Conflict-Affected and High-Risk Areas," which includes a five-step framework for risk-based due diligence in the supply chain.[20] According to the release, the regulation gives EU importers an opportunity to deepen ongoing efforts to ensure clean supply chains when trading legitimately with operators in conflict-affected countries.

---

[18]The mandate of the force intervention brigade was renewed by the UN Security Council until March 2015.

[19]Canada also has a proposed conflict minerals initiative. According to State, Canada's Conflict Minerals Act was reintroduced for discussion in the Canadian parliament in April 2014 and would require Canadian companies to exercise due diligence in respect of the exploitation and trading of designated conflict minerals originating in the Great Lakes Region of Africa.

[20]The OECD due diligence guidance, which OECD adopted in 2011, includes supplements on tin, tantalum, tungsten, and gold. The framework's five steps are (1) establishing strong company management systems, (2) identifying and assessing risk in the supply chain, (3) designing and implementing a strategy to respond to identified risks, (4) carrying out an independent third-party audit of supply chain due diligence at identified points in the supply chain, and (5) reporting on supply chain due diligence. Organization for Economic Cooperation and Development, *OECD Due Diligence Guidance for Responsible Supply Chains of Minerals from Conflict-Affected and High-Risk Areas: Second Edition*, OECD Publishing (2013), accessed June 23, 2014, http://dx.doi.org/10.1787/9789264185050-en.

Conflict Minerals Supply Chains

Uses of Conflict Minerals

Various industries, particularly manufacturing industries, use the four conflict minerals in a wide variety of products. For example, tin is used to solder metal pieces and is also found in food packaging, in steel coatings on automobile parts, and in some plastics. Most tantalum is used to manufacture tantalum capacitors, which enable energy storage in electronic products such as cell phones and computers as well as used to produce alloy additives, which can be found in turbines in jet engines. Tungsten is used in automobile manufacturing, drill bits and cutting tools, and other industrial manufacturing tools and is the primary component of filaments in light bulbs. Gold is used as reserves and in jewelry and is also used by the electronics industry.

Source: GAO-12-763. | GAO-14-575

Supply chains for companies using tin, tantalum, tungsten, and gold generally begin at the mine site, where ore is extracted from the ground with mechanized or artisanal mining techniques.[21] However, these supply chains can be complex and vary considerably, according to some industry association and company representatives. For example, as figure 2 shows, in the "upstream" segment of the supply chain—that is, from mine to smelter—ore may be purchased by a local processor or trader and then by an exporter, who ships it to a smelter for refinement; in other cases, the ore may be sold directly to an exporter. The "downstream" segments of conflict mineral supply chains—that is, from smelter to manufacturer—may vary as well, depending in part on the type of mineral. Figure 2 provides a simplified depiction of the supply chain for the four conflict minerals.

Figure 2: Simplified Conflict Minerals Supply Chain

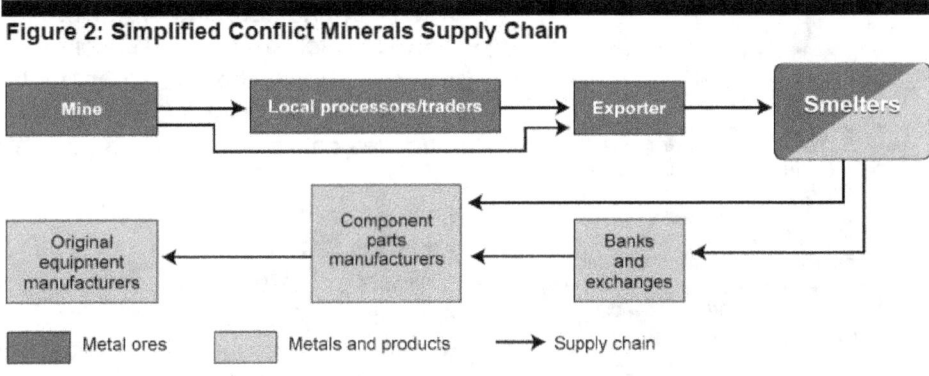

Source: GAO analysis. | GAO-14-575

Smelters and refiners are considered the "choke points" in the supply chain, since a limited number of smelters and refiners process conflict minerals worldwide and the origin of the minerals after processing can be difficult to verify. Smelters primarily provide high-purity tin, tantalum, and tungsten directly to component parts manufacturers, although some sell high-purity metals through traders or exchanges. Gold refiners typically sell high-purity gold to banks for use as a store of value or to international exchanges where gold is bought and sold,[22] although some refiners sell

---

[21]Artisanal mining is a form of mining characterized by a lack of mechanization or capital investment.

[22]According to a World Gold Council representative, in most cases refiners are paid a fee to refine gold and the transaction is conducted by the miner, the trader, and the bank.

gold directly to manufacturers; banks and traders may also sell gold to manufacturers, including jewelry and component parts manufacturers. Component parts manufacturers use the refined tin, tantalum, tungsten, or gold to construct individual parts—such as capacitors, engine parts, or clasps for necklaces—that they sell to original equipment manufacturers. The original equipment manufacturers complete the final assembly of a product and sell the final product to the consumer.

Responsible Sourcing Initiatives

Global and In-Region Sourcing Initiatives

Global sourcing initiatives may minimize the risk that minerals that have been exploited by illegal armed groups will enter the supply chain and may also support companies' efforts to identify the source of the conflict minerals across the supply chain around the world. In-region sourcing initiatives may support responsible sourcing of conflict minerals from Central Africa and the identification of specific mines of origin for those minerals. Such initiatives in DRC and adjoining countries focus on tracing minerals from the mine to the mineral smelter or refiner by supporting a bagging and tagging program or some type of traceability scheme.

Source: GAO | GAO-14-575

Various stakeholders—including governments, industry associations, international organizations, and international and local NGOs working in the Great Lakes Region—operate or support initiatives to promote and exercise responsible sourcing of conflict minerals. Stakeholder-developed initiatives—which include the development of guidance documents, audit protocols, and sourcing practices—support efforts by companies reporting to SEC under the rule to (1) conduct due diligence of their conflict minerals supply chain, (2) identify the source of conflict minerals within their supply chain, and (3) responsibly source conflict minerals. The initiatives can be divided into two categories: global or in-region.[23]

Most responsible sourcing initiatives follow OECD's due-diligence guidance.[24] The guidance is for use by any company potentially sourcing minerals or metals from conflict-affected and high-risk areas and, according to OECD, is one of the only international frameworks available to help companies meet their due diligence reporting requirements.

---

[23]See GAO-12-763.

[24]Organization for Economic Cooperation and Development, *OECD Due Diligence Guidance for Responsible Supply Chains of Minerals from Conflict-Affected and High-Risk Areas: Second Edition* (Paris: November 2012).

U.S. Agencies Have Taken Actions Related to Responsible Sourcing of Conflict Minerals, but Commerce Has Not Yet Fulfilled Its Requirements

Since the Act was passed in 2010, State, USAID, SEC, and Commerce have undertaken activities related to implementation of the Act's conflict minerals provisions, including activities related to responsible sourcing of such minerals from the DRC and adjoining countries. As required by the Act, State and USAID developed a strategy in 2011 aimed at addressing the linkages between human rights abuses, armed groups, the mining of conflict minerals, and commercial products and are implementing various objectives of the strategy. State also produced a map of mineral-rich areas under control of armed groups in the DRC. SEC issued its required conflict minerals rule in 2012. As of May 2014, Commerce had taken steps toward producing a list of all conflict minerals processing facilities worldwide, which the Act required by January 2013, but had not completed the task. Moreover, Commerce had not developed a plan of action with associated timeframes for how and when it expects to complete this effort and report to Congress. Standard practices in program and project management and execution include, among other things, developing a plan to execute specific projects needed to obtain defined results within a specific time frame.[25] State, USAID, SEC, and Commerce also have engaged in activities involving stakeholder partnerships and outreach and have provided technical assistance to other governments related to activities focused on the responsible sourcing of conflict minerals.

State, USAID, and SEC Have Addressed the Act's Requirements, and Commerce Is Working toward Fulfilling Its Requirements

The Act directed State, USAID, SEC, and Commerce to undertake various activities to implement its provisions related to conflict minerals. Since the Act was passed in 2010, the agencies have taken the following actions.

State and USAID Developed a Strategy, and State Produced a Conflict Minerals Map

Responding to the Act, State and USAID developed a strategy in 2011 to address the linkages among human rights abuses, armed groups, the mining of conflict minerals, and commercial products. The Act required State and USAID to submit, by January 2011,[26] a strategy to address the

---

[25]The Project Management Institute, *The Standard for Program Management* (2013).

[26]The Act states that a strategy be submitted to Congress no later than 180 days after the enactment of the law.

linkages between human rights abuses, armed groups, mining of conflict minerals, and commercial products. The strategy document that State and USAID submitted to Congress in 2011 lists five objectives: (1) promote an appropriate role of security forces, (2) enhance civilian regulation of minerals trade in the DRC, (3) protect artisanal miners and local communities, (4) strengthen regional and international efforts, and (5) promote due diligence and responsible trade through public outreach. The strategy includes activities corresponding with each of these objectives—for example, building the capacity of civilian mining authorities in the DRC to certify mine sites, supporting the implementation and coordination of certification and traceability schemes, building the capacity of the ICGLR related to mineral audit mechanisms, and engaging with industries and civil society groups regarding supply chain due diligence efforts. State and USAID officials indicated that they have been implementing objectives of the strategy over the past few years. According to the U.S. Special Envoy for the Great Lakes Region and the DRC, the strategy remains relevant and accurate and State has used it in conjunction with other U.S. government agencies as a roadmap for efforts to help break the link between armed groups and conflict minerals.

In addition, in 2011, State developed a map of mineral-rich zones and areas under control of armed groups in the DRC and has subsequently published several updated maps, as required by the Act.[27] The maps are focused on the exploitation of tin, tantalum, tungsten, and gold in the provinces of North and South Kivu and parts of Orientale, Maniema, and Katanga provinces. According to State, the most current map, which State published in February 2014, was based on data from surveys conducted in 2013 by the International Peace Information Service (IPIS)—an NGO— and on information from consultations with the DRC government, the UN Group of Experts, and MONUSCO (see app. II for the 2014 map).[28] State reported that lack of complete or fully verifiable data makes it difficult to confirm the location of many mine sites, to establish which mine sites are active at any given time, and to comprehensively verify reports of armed groups or other entities that are

---

[27]The Act requires that State should update its map every 180 days.

[28]IPIS has also published a report that analyzes the information it collects and populates in its interactive map. See International Peace Information Service, *Analysis of the Interactive Map of Artisanal Mining Areas in Eastern DR Congo,* (Antwerp, Belgium: November 2013), accessed June 23, 2014, http://ipisresearch.be/mapping/webmapping/drcongo.

either present at mines or have access to revenue streams emanating from them. State officials indicated that in the future the map may become digital rather than paper based.

SEC Issued Its Conflict Minerals Rule in 2012

As we previously reported,[29] SEC issued its conflict minerals rule in August 2012.[30] The Act required that SEC promulgate, by April 2011, disclosure and reporting regulations regarding the use of conflict minerals from the DRC and adjoining countries.[31]

---

[29]GAO-13-689.

[30]In October 2012, the U.S. Chamber of Commerce, the National Association of Manufacturers, and the Business Roundtable filed a lawsuit against SEC challenging the final conflict minerals rule, making claims based on the Administrative Procedure Act, the Securities Exchange Act of 1934, and the First Amendment. In July 2013, the U.S. District Court for the District of Columbia denied the plaintiff's claims on all counts. See *National Association of Manufacturers v. SEC*, 956 F. Supp. 2d 43 (D.D.C. 2013). In August 2013, the petitioners appealed the decision to the U.S. Court of Appeals for the District of Columbia Circuit, and on April 14, 2014, the appeals court upheld the District Court's findings on all the petitioners' claims except the First Amendment claims, concluding that section 13(p) of the Exchange Act and the final conflicts minerals rule violate the First Amendment "to the extent the statute and rule require regulated entities to report to the Commission and to state on their website that any of their products have 'not been found to be DRC conflict free.'" *National Association of Manufacturers, et al. v. SEC et al., No. 13-5252 (D.C. Cir. April 14, 2014)*. In response to the appeals court's findings, SEC staff, on April 29, 2014, issued a statement that it expects companies to file any reports required under Rule 13p-1 subject to any further action that may be taken either by the Commission or a court. The SEC staff's statement contains guidance to companies, which provides, among other things, that no company is required to describe its products (1) as "DRC conflict free" (2) as having "not been found to be 'DRC conflict free'," or (3) as "DRC conflict undeterminable" in their reports. The guidance also states that a company may voluntarily elect to describe any of its products as "DRC conflict free" in its report if it had obtained an independent private sector audit as required by the rule. In addition, the guidance states that, pending further action, an independent private sector audit will not be required unless a company voluntarily elects to describe a product as "DRC conflict free" in its Conflict Minerals Report. On May 2, 2014, the SEC issued an order staying the effective date for compliance with the portions of Rule 13p-1 and Form SD subject to the appeals court's First Amendment holding pending the completion of judicial review. On May 5, 2014, the plaintiffs filed a motion with the appeals court asking the court to stay the entire rule pending the completion of judicial review which the Commission opposed, and on May 2014, the appeals court denied the motion.

[31]Pub. L. No. 111-203, sec 1502(b). The Act required that a rule should be promulgated no later than 270 days after the law's enactment. As we reported in 2012, SEC's issuance of the rule encountered delays, including delays in developing, modifying, and finalizing the rule, as a result of several factors. See GAO-12-763. Also see appendix III for a flowchart summarizing the conflict minerals rule that SEC published when the rule was adopted in 2012.

SEC issued a "frequently asked questions" (FAQ) document in May 2013 to address questions by companies that will have to report to SEC under the conflict minerals rule. SEC officials indicated that these FAQs included questions posed most often by companies regarding interpretation of the rule. In April 2014, SEC issued additional FAQs addressing questions that mostly pertained to the independent private sector audit of companies' conflict minerals disclosure reports. According to an SEC official, these FAQs were based on interpretive questions asked by SEC-reporting companies and the audit community.

In January 2014, SEC made "Form SD," a specialized disclosure form for reporting compliance with the conflict minerals rule, available for electronic filing. The form, originally published with the conflict minerals rule, provides general instructions to SEC-reporting companies for filing the conflict minerals disclosure and specifies the information that their conflict minerals reports must include. SEC-reporting companies were required to file under the rule for the first time by June 2, 2014, and annually thereafter on May 31.[32] According to SEC officials, based on preliminary feedback they received, they anticipated that most SEC-reporting companies subject to the rule would be unable to determine whether or not their products qualified as "DRC conflict-free."[33]

Commerce Has Taken Steps but Has Not Provided a List of Conflict Minerals Processing Facilities to Congress

More than a year after the deadline required by the Act, Commerce has not yet fulfilled its mandate under section 1502 of the Act. Section 1502 directed Commerce to report, among other things, a list of all known conflict minerals processing facilities worldwide to appropriate congressional committees annually starting no later than 30 months after

---

[32]The SEC rule indicates that if the deadline for filing the conflict mineral disclosure report occurs on a weekend, or on a holiday which the SEC is not open for business, then the deadline shall be the next business day.

[33]According to the rule, for a temporary period following the effective date of the rule—4 years for smaller reporting companies or 2 years for all other reporting companies—if a company is unable to determine whether the minerals in its products originated in DRC or the adjoining countries or financed or benefited armed groups in those countries, then those products are considered "DRC conflict undeterminable" and no audit is required. According to SEC officials, as a result of the SEC's partial stay order and the SEC staff's statement, companies are not required to describe their products in their reports as "DRC conflict undeterminable" pending further action by the SEC or a court, and no audits are required unless a company voluntarily describes any of its products as "DRC conflict free" in its Conflict Minerals Report.

the Act's enactment—that is, by January 2013.[34] As of May 2014, Commerce had not developed such a list or developed a plan of action, with associated time frames, for completing this requirement and reporting it to Congress. Standard practices in program and project management include developing, among other things, a program plan to execute specific projects needed to obtain defined programmatic results within a specific time frame. In January 2014, Commerce officials told us that they had identified entities that they hoped would help them identify publicly available information about conflict minerals and identify stakeholders who are knowledgeable about conflict minerals issues. Specifically, Commerce officials indicated that they had assembled a proposed and internal outreach plan, which includes meeting with stakeholders to discuss how these organizations have gathered information on conflict mineral smelters and identifies other efforts that Commerce can explore to develop the list of conflict minerals processing facilities. Commerce officials also indicated that they anticipated a 3- to 4-month time frame for the proposed outreach efforts to talk to stakeholders. In May 2014, Commerce officials stated that they had completed discussions with the majority of the stakeholders identified in the outreach plan and have developed several preliminary lists of conflict minerals processing facilities, based on information they obtained from the stakeholders. However, Commerce officials stated that they did not have a timeframe for completing the final list for Congress.

Commerce officials said that they had encountered some challenges associated with gathering data on conflict minerals to help inform their outreach plan and required reporting. For example, according to the officials, conflict minerals and mining operations are difficult to track; because the equipment used to process conflict minerals can be moved easily, such operations can emerge in different locations. In addition, Commerce officials mentioned that some conflict minerals data may be inaccessible to the U.S. government because a large number of conflict

---

[34]The Act also requires Commerce to annually report (1) an assessment of the accuracy of the independent private sector audits and other due diligence processes required under section 1502 and (2) recommendations for the processes to carry out such audits, including ways to improve the accuracy of the audits and to establish standards of best practices. Commerce officials stated that it was unable to implement these aspects of the Act's requirement because the SEC disclosure reports, which are needed for the assessment, were not due to SEC until June 2, 2014.

mineral smelters are in China.[35] Having an action plan with associated timeframes could better position Commerce to report on the status of its efforts to compile a list of conflict minerals processing facilities worldwide and to hold its personnel accountable for completing its related activities.

Some stakeholders that we contacted, including government and industry officials and representatives of the UN Group of Experts and an NGO, indicated that a comprehensive list of conflict minerals smelters and refiners—considered the "choke point" of the supply chain—would be very useful in the effort to ensure responsible sourcing of minerals in the DRC and adjoining countries. According to these stakeholders, such a list would enable companies that are subject to the SEC rule to maintain transparency regarding their supply chains, particularly in their communications with smelters, and would also provide companies the information they need for their SEC-required conflict minerals disclosure reports.

U.S. Agencies Have Engaged in Partnerships and Outreach and Provided Technical Assistance to Stakeholders

U.S. government agencies have engaged in a variety of activities that involve partnerships and coordination with other stakeholders or outreach to stakeholders, and some agencies have provided technical assistance to stakeholders regarding responsible sourcing of conflict minerals. Some agencies' activities contribute to global and in-region responsible sourcing initiatives and some of the activities address the implementation of objectives outlined in the strategy to address the linkages between human rights abuses, armed groups, and the mining of conflict minerals.

U.S. Agency Partnerships and Coordination Efforts

Some U.S. agencies have partnered and coordinated with other stakeholders—other government agencies, industry, and civil society—regarding issues related to responsible sourcing of conflict minerals. For example:

- State and USAID, both in headquarters and posts or missions overseas, and other U.S. agencies coordinate with one another on weekly or biweekly conference calls to discuss the progress of responsible sourcing efforts, provide updates on recent events, and collaborate on future events, according to State and USAID officials.

---

[35]Our 2013 report identified 82 smelters and refiners of tin, tantalum, tungsten, and gold located in China, of the 278 smelters and refiners that we identified worldwide.

- USAID works in a collaborative and coordinated manner with State in Washington and regionally, using the 2011 U.S. strategy as a framework for the coordination, according to USAID officials. The officials indicated that funding also has been coordinated between the two agencies across the five objectives of the strategy and totals over $25 million, as of 2013.
- State and USAID coordinate with other stakeholders through the Public-Private Alliance for Responsible Minerals Trade (PPA) to fund and support organizations working on responsible sourcing efforts. Both State and USAID are on the PPA's Governance Committee, which consists of participants from foreign governments, industry, and civil society.[36]
- USAID has partnered with the International Organization for Migration to help enhance civilian control of the DRC's mineral trade through infrastructure improvements and institutional reforms, according to agency officials. The officials reported that with USAID funding, the organization will also establish pilot certification and traceability systems in and around the mineral trading centers and other areas of South and North Kivu.[37]
- USAID has partnered and coordinated with stakeholders in the DRC, according to agency officials. For example, the officials said that USAID is coordinating with the DRC government regarding various aspects of minerals trade, is involved in the multi-stakeholder Mining Thematic Group in the DRC, and facilitates the Eastern Congo Mining Coordination Team.
- On a multilateral level, both USAID and State participate in the OECD Responsible Sourcing Stakeholder Forums held every 6 months, according to USAID officials. This forum, coordinated by the ICGLR, OECD, and the UN Group of Experts, is a platform for governments, the private sector, international organizations, and civil society to share experiences with implementation of supply chain due diligence for responsible sourcing of minerals from conflict-affected and high-

---

[36]According to USAID, it holds two of the four government positions on the Committee in addition to State and the ICGLR. There are four civil society and four private sector members of the Committee as well.

[37]According to an NGO report, the objective of mineral trading centers, or *centre de negoce*, is to provide a center where miners and traders can do business without interference from armed groups. The report notes that, at the same time, state agents can exert control and levy taxes, traders can receive the necessary paperwork, and miners can profit from a market environment in which they can negotiate better prices for their products.

risk areas. Both State and USAID officials have participated at times as facilitators of these forums.

- The current U.S. Special Envoy for the Great Lakes Region and the DRC has collaborated with other stakeholders, such as the UN Special Envoy for the Great Lakes, the African Union, and other multilateral and bilateral partners, to strengthen international coordination mechanisms on the crisis in the Great Lakes, according to State. These efforts have taken place under the Peace, Security, and Cooperation Framework Agreement for the DRC and the Region.

U.S. Agency Outreach Efforts

A couple of U.S. government agencies indicated that they have conducted outreach to various stakeholders to promote responsible sourcing of conflict minerals and to obtain information about conflict mineral sourcing and supply chains. For example, State and Commerce officials reported the following.

- State officials told us that State has engaged with foreign governments and industry associations regarding the Dodd-Frank Act requirements. According to these officials, State's efforts have included sending letters about section 1502 of the Act to foreign governments that are prominent in the conflict mineral supply chain as well as encouraging these governments and companies in those countries to support the aim of the legislation. In a November 2013 briefing, the Deputy Assistant Secretary of State for Counter Threat Finance and Sanctions reported that he had travelled to Asia and Europe to talk with representatives from smelters and governments about responsible sourcing initiatives and encourage participation in such initiatives. State officials also indicated that they have facilitated outreach efforts for industry associations, such as the Conflict-Free Smelter Initiative (CFSI) and others, to help them secure meetings in Asian countries to discuss conflict free mining and smelting. According to the State officials, during the outreach some members from industry and industry associations expressed interest in talking to Commerce about smelters and support for responsible sourcing, according to State officials.
- Commerce officials stated that their proposed outreach plan identified entities that could enable them to develop the list of conflict mineral smelters and refiners required by the Act. According to these officials, they have conducted outreach to these entities, including government agencies, industry associations, international organizations, and NGOs.

U.S. Agency Technical Assistance

Some U.S. agencies have provided technical assistance related to responsible sourcing of conflict minerals to various stakeholders. According to agency officials, these stakeholders have consisted primarily of other governments, particularly in the Great Lakes Region. For example:

- State officials said that they had shared experiences and challenges related to implementing the Act with officials from the EU who were working on proposed conflict minerals legislation.
- SEC officials stated that they had discussed with EU officials issues that SEC considered when drafting the conflict minerals rule as well as questions about the rule that SEC received from industry.
- USAID officials stated that they had been working with the ICGLR in providing technical assistance on conflict minerals programs, particularly through the steering committee for ICGLR's Regional Initiative against the Illegal Exploitation of Natural Resources.[38] Specifically, according to USAID officials, USAID has been implementing a multiyear institutional capacity program in support of the ICGLR to build the overall strength of the Executive Secretariat as well as the ICGLR's regional initiative. USAID officials said that the agency will soon begin implementing activities to support a third-party supply chain audit mechanism and an independent conflict minerals supply chain auditor.

Stakeholder Initiatives Are Expanding and Provide Some Information on Sourcing of Conflict Minerals

Since we reported in July 2013,[39] stakeholders have expanded existing initiatives and added new initiatives focused on responsible sourcing of conflict minerals in the DRC and adjoining countries, to include new mine sites, countries, and smelters. Some of these initiatives have yielded publically available information, including data on production of conflict-free minerals and export data, as well as reports on the progress and results of the initiatives. However, this information is limited in scope and thus may not provide a comprehensive description of the sourcing of conflict minerals from the DRC and adjoining countries.

---

[38]The Regional Steering Committee, comprising technical experts from all ICGLR member states, has been charged with the steering of all activities within the initiative since September 2009. Its suggestions on policies and technical guidelines are to be approved at a later stage by the Regional Inter-Ministerial Committee as well as the ICGLR Summit.

[39]GAO-13-689.

Stakeholders Have Expanded Existing Initiatives, and New Initiatives Are Underway

Stakeholders have recently expanded, or made plans to expand, a number of existing global and in-region responsible sourcing initiatives; and two new initiatives are underway. Figure 3 shows the starting dates for existing, expanding, and new responsible sourcing initiatives. According to some stakeholders we interviewed, improvement in security in eastern DRC and industries' growing awareness of responsible sourcing and the Act's requirements may account for the expansion of responsible sourcing initiative.

Figure 3: Timeline of the Starting Dates of Stakeholder-led Initiatives from 2008 to June 2014

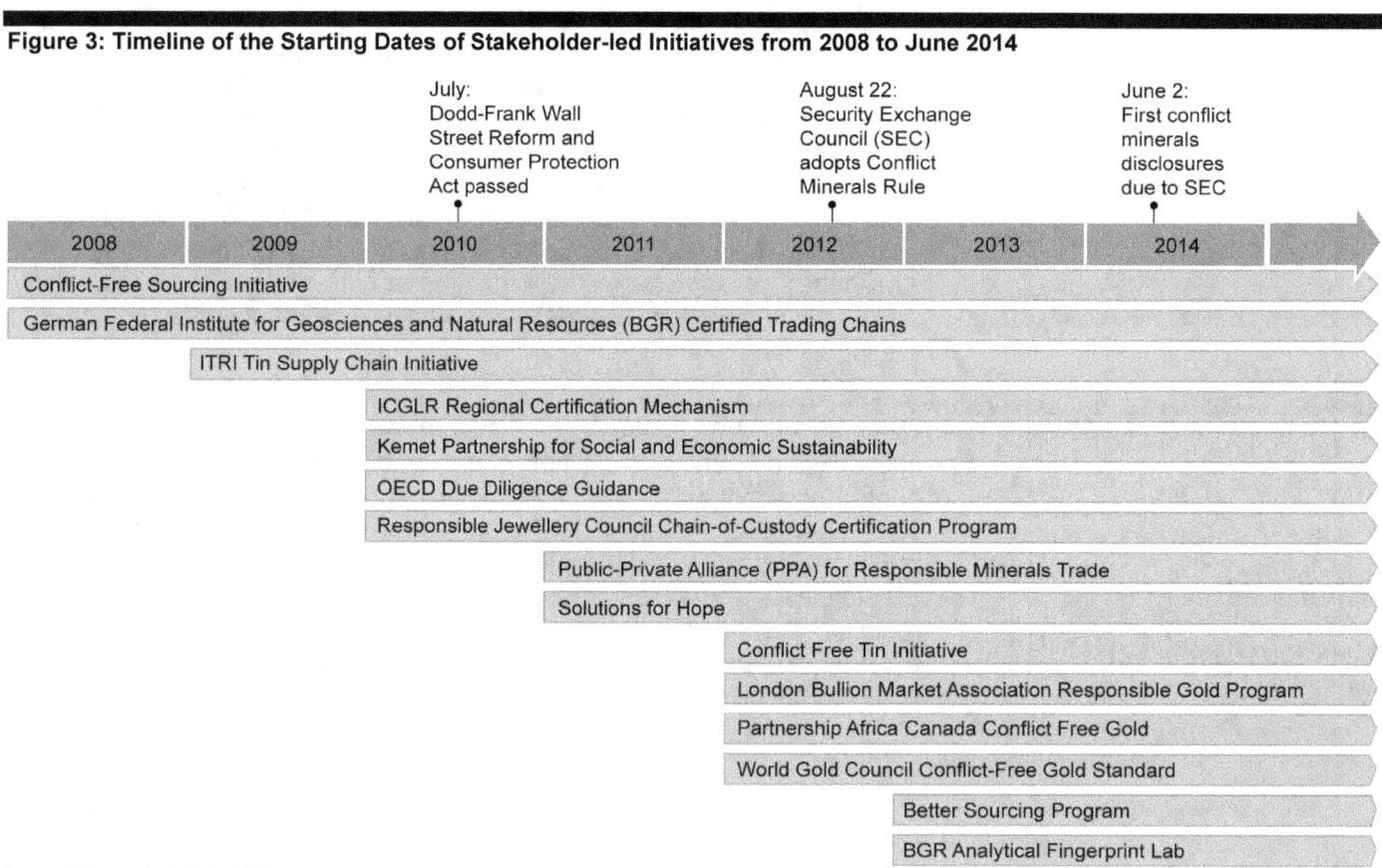

Source: GAO analysis. | GAO-14-575

| Some Existing Global Initiatives Are Expanding | The following are examples of global responsible-sourcing initiatives that stakeholders have expanded since we reported in July 2013.[40] |

Conflict-Free Sourcing Initiative

The Conflict-Free Sourcing Initiative (CFSI) has expanded in several aspects related to responsible sourcing.[41] First, CFSI's Conflict-Free Smelter Program has expanded the number of smelters it has certified as conflict free. The program is a voluntary one in which smelters undergo an independent third-party audit, in accordance with OECD's due diligence guidelines, to verify the origin of minerals processed at their facilities. The number of smelters that the program has certified as conflict-free has expanded from 26 smelters in summer 2013 to 85 smelters as of April 25, 2014 (see table 1). An additional 25 smelters are in the process of being certified, bringing the total number of smelters involved in the program to 110.[42] As of January 2014, the Conflict-Free Smelter Program has expanded to include smelters for tungsten in addition to the other three conflict minerals.

Table 1: Number of Smelters and Refiners in the Conflict-Free Smelter Program as of April 25, 2014

Mineral	Number of certified smelters/refiners	Number of smelters/refiners working toward certification	Total
Tantalum	28	1	29
Tin	13	14	27
Tungsten	1	8	9
Gold	43	2	45
Total	**85**	**25**	**110**

Source: Conflict-Free Sourcing Initiative data, GAO (analysis). | GAO-14-575

[40]GAO-13-689.

[41]CFSI was founded in 2008 by members of the Electronic Industry Citizenship Coalition (EICC) and the Global e-Sustainability Initiative (GeSI). According to EICC and GeSI, as of April 30, 2013, CFSI now includes EICC and GeSI activities and is an expanded initiative of the EICC and GeSI Extractives Working Group, which includes more stakeholders and a wider range of industry sectors supporting the sourcing of conflict-free minerals.

[42]The actual number of smelters and refiners of conflict minerals is unknown. However, in 2013, we reported that the total number of smelters and refiners worldwide could be as high as 500. See GAO-13-689.

Second, according to CFSI representatives, through outreach to industry, CFSI has expanded its collaboration with companies involved with the conflict minerals supply chain. CFSI's outreach includes twice-yearly workshops on conflict minerals issues that are open to all participants. According to CFSI, outreach such as these workshops bring together hundreds of representatives from industry, government, and civil society for updates, in-depth discussions, and guidance on best practices for responsible mineral sourcing.[43] CFSI officials stated that such outreach recently resulted in collaboration with the tungsten industry, which led to certification of the first conflict-free tungsten smelter in 2014.

Third, in 2014, CFSI began offering its members information about the SEC-required "reasonable country of origin" data for conflict minerals, providing the most detailed information currently available about the source of conflict minerals for smelting and refining facilities that are validated through the Conflict-Free Smelter Program. According to CFSI, this information may be useful to companies as they prepare the conflict minerals disclosure reports required by the SEC rule and demonstrate conformance with the OECD due diligence guidelines.

Responsible Gold Program

In January 2012, the London Bullion Market Association (LBMA), which represents the global market for gold and silver, finalized and published its Responsible Gold Guidance to ensure that the gold refiners it accredits purchase only conflict-free gold.[44] The refiners accredited by LBMA are required to complete an annual third-party audit to verify their compliance with the LBMA guidance, according to an LBMA official. As of March 2014, of the 67 gold refiners that LBMA oversees, more than three-quarters had successfully submitted their audits and received the Responsible Gold Certificate, according to the official. The representative stated that if a refiner does not submit a third-party audit by the end of

---

[43]The World Bank defines "civil society" as referring to the wide array of nongovernmental and not-for-profit organizations that have a presence in public life, expressing the interests and values of their members or others, based on ethical, cultural, political, scientific, religious, or philanthropic considerations.

[44]LBMA oversees the London Good Delivery List, a list of 67 accredited gold refiners that meet a specific standard for the quality of their refined gold and silver bars. According to LBMA representatives, most banks and exchanges will only contract with refiners on the Good Delivery List.

GAO-14-575 Conflict Minerals

2014, the refiner will be removed from LBMA's list of accredited refiners. An LBMA official said that the association also collaborates with other responsible sourcing stakeholders and global gold exchanges and works closely with OECD. For example, the official said that, working through OECD, LBMA has met with Chinese industry representatives to clarify the purpose and benefits of conducting due diligence audits of their refiners.

Responsible Jewellery Council Chain-of-Custody Certification Program

The Responsible Jewellery Council—a diamond and precious metals industry association—launched a chain-of-custody certification program in March 2012 to help its member companies identify and track conflict-free gold throughout their supply chains.[45] The program's requirements, which are aligned with the OECD Due Diligence Guidance for gold, include a third-party audit of each certified entity to ensure that its gold is conflict-free, according to the Responsible Jewellery Council. According to an official with the Responsible Jewellery Council, this certification can support companies' compliance with the Dodd Frank Act. As of April 2014, nine entities had been validated under the council's certification program and more entities were in the process of being certified, according to the official.[46]

Some In-Region Initiatives Have Also Expanded

The following are examples of in-region responsible sourcing initiatives that stakeholders have expanded, or made plans to expand, since we reported in July 2013.

---

[45]The Responsible Jewellery Council launched its chain-of-custody program to also help its member companies identify and track the supply chains of other precious metals, such as platinum, palladium, and rhodium. Chain of custody refers to the paper trail that documents the sequence of entities with custody of minerals as they move through a supply chain.

[46]Officials of the Responsible Jewellery Council reported that the council has developed cross-recognition agreements with CFSI, LBMA, and the World Gold Council to reduce unnecessary duplicative audits for their member companies. For example, according to an LBMA official, once LBMA approves a third-party audit, verifying that a gold refiner is conflict-free, the association contacts CFSI to add the refiner to CFSI's list of compliant smelters and refiners.

ITRI Tin Supply Chain Initiative

The ITRI Tin Supply Chain Initiative (iTSCi) recently announced that it is expanding its in-region operations. The initiative works with "upstream" entities (i.e., companies involved in the conflict minerals supply chain from mine to smelter) in instituting the actions, structures, and processes necessary to conform with the OECD Due Diligence Guidance and helps relevant U.S. companies report on their due diligence efforts to the SEC as required by the Dodd-Frank Act.[47] The assistance that iTSCi provides includes a system to trace bags of minerals from the mines to the exporter, due diligence audits of iTSCi's member companies, and assessments of the political and security situations, which have been conducted at various mine sites in the DRC and Rwanda.

In February 2014, iTSCi announced that it was expanding its traceability program into a remote area in the northern region of the Maniema province of the DRC, and into the North Kivu province of the DRC. According to iTSCi, improved security in North Kivu, which has a history of armed conflict, accounts in part for the expansion into the province. An iTSCi official stated that the initiative is currently looking at options for extending into South Kivu. Additionally, in April 2014, iTSCi announced that the program had started operations in Burundi. According to iTSCi, there is presently little evidence of activity by nongovernment armed groups in Burundi, since there have been no reports that armed groups are controlling mine sites or transportation routes, extorting money or minerals, or illegally taxing the trade of minerals. iTSCi further reported that it may extend the program to Uganda and eventually to the entire Great Lakes Region. Also, an iTSCi official stated that the initiative had successfully piloted technology in Rwanda to collect and manage data on conflict minerals electronically, which would replace the current paper-based system and increase efficiency of data collection.

---

[47]According to iTSCi, as of November 2013, the traceability program is used at more than 850 mines in the South Kivu, Maniema, and Katanga provinces of the DRC and in Rwanda. Almost all in-region responsible sourcing initiatives—including Solutions for Hope and the Conflict-Free Tin Initiative—use iTSCi's traceability system of tracking minerals from the mine to the exporter to ensure that their minerals are conflict-free.

Solutions for Hope

Launched by Motorola Solutions and AVX in 2011, the Solutions for Hope tantalum program is a "closed-pipeline" initiative that traces the flow of tantalum from the mine to the end-use company.[48] In June 2013, Solutions for Hope reported that it had completed six shipments of tantalum, totaling more than 145 metric tons, from the Katanga province in the DRC. According to officials, in part because of improved security in the province, the initiative started sourcing tantalum from North Kivu in March 2014. Officials also noted that Solutions for Hope is exploring a closed pipeline system for gold in the DRC.

Conflict-Free Tin Initiative

The Conflict-Free Tin Initiative (CFTI), a multistakeholder effort supported by the Netherlands government, is a closed-pipeline initiative, similar to Solutions for Hope, started in October 2012 for sourcing tin from the South Kivu province of the DRC. According to CFTI, the initiative has expanded its mining operation to Maniema, a province bordering South Kivu, which is less prone to conflict and the government is reinvesting tax income into the mining communities. According to USAID, a CFTI stakeholder, from October 2012 to December 2013, the initiative generated a total export value of more than $3 million.

Regional Certification Mechanism

In 2010, the International Conference on the Great Lakes Region (ICGLR) began working with an NGO to develop a regional certification mechanism to ensure that conflict minerals are fully traceable. ICGLR's Regional Certification Mechanism (RCM) enables member countries and their mining companies to demonstrate where and under what conditions minerals were produced, allowing member governments to issue ICGLR regional certificates for those mineral shipments that are in compliance with the standards of the mechanism. The ICGLR issued its first certificate in November 2013 to a mine in Rwanda. According to an ICGLR official, the DRC launched its certificate program but had not yet issued any certificates as of November 2013. He added that Tanzania

---

[48]According to Solutions for Hope, its closed pipeline involved working through a defined set of key suppliers—mines (including artisanal cooperatives), smelter/processor, component manufacturer, and end user—identified in advance of initiating the project.

and Burundi may be able to issue certificates by the end of 2014. The ICGLR official noted several challenges in instituting the RCM in the DRC and the region. For example, he cited that it is logistically difficult to catalogue all mines in each country. In addition, the official noted that training local officials to use the RCM software is difficult and time consuming. The official added that it takes member countries 1 year to prepare for all components associated with launching the RCM.

New Initiatives Have Launched in the Region Since 2013

In the past year, one existing stakeholder has launched a new in-region responsible sourcing initiative and a new stakeholder has established an initiative.

Analytical Fingerprint Project

The German government's Federal Institute for Geosciences and Natural Resources (BGR), an existing stakeholder, launched a new initiative in the past year. According to a representative, BGR's primary role is to support the region's governments and to build government capacity. Since 2013, BGR has initiated the Analytical Fingerprint Project to allow for independent verification of the origin of the conflict mineral by comparing the composition of tantalum, tin, and tungsten concentrate samples of a known origin with unknown samples, similar to a DNA test. According to a BGR official, the project has three types of units—sample preparation labs, high tech labs, and a management unit. To date, BGR has established sample preparation labs, located in Rwanda since 2013 and in the DRC since 2014, where mineral ore samples are prepared for analysis. A third sample preparation lab is under construction in Burundi. BGR is in negotiations to establish a high tech lab in Tanzania, which receives and analyzes the samples from the preparation labs. Additionally, in 2013, according to a BGR official, BGR established a project management unit at the ICGLR headquarters in Burundi, which evaluates the raw data and produces the analytical fingerprints.

Better Sourcing Program Responsible-Sourcing Pilot

The Better Sourcing Program (BSP), a private company that offers an independently audited due diligence assurance program to enable companies to source tantalum, tin, tungsten, and gold from the region, is a new stakeholder in the region in 2013. The Better Sourcing Program established a pilot program that covers a tantalum supply chain originating from the Republic of the Congo (also known as Congo-Brazzaville), which is the first responsible-sourcing initiative in that country. Better Sourcing Program officials stated that they chose to pilot the initiative in the Republic of the Congo because no other scheme to support producers existed there, because the country is relatively conflict free, and because the government has been cooperative.

Stakeholders Face Operational Challenges in Expanding or Launching In-Region Initiatives

Some stakeholders that we interviewed noted various challenges to expanding or launching responsible-sourcing efforts in the DRC and adjoining countries. For example:

- **Lack of infrastructure.** Some stakeholders reported that inadequate infrastructure in the DRC and adjoining countries affects their ability to operate in the region and expand initiatives to new areas. Representatives from Solutions for Hope stated that infrastructure in the DRC cannot support a large-scale smelter. According to these representatives, the power supply in the DRC can be inconsistent and, because smelting facilities require a large, consistent power supply to function properly, all tin, tantalum, and tungsten currently are exported from the DRC and Rwanda for smelting.[49]
- **Lack of government support.** Some stakeholders reported some operational challenges related to the region's national and provincial governments. For example, stakeholders involved in the Conflict Free Tin Initiative stated that sales of tin from their mine in South Kivu were halted for nearly 2 months in 2013 after the provincial government of the region imposed harsh taxes on the minerals mined there. Additionally, Solutions for Hope officials reported that the DRC's current tax structure is not conducive to legitimizing gold and that expanding the initiative to include gold is therefore difficult.
- **Lack of buyers for conflict minerals from conflict zones.** Several stakeholders and agency officials reported that some companies are reluctant to buy minerals produced in the DRC and adjoining countries because of the high cost of the due diligence required by the Dodd-Frank Act and the perceived reputational risk. For example, according to one industry official, a major challenge to responsible sourcing in the region is that the cost of complying with the SEC rule makes it difficult for SEC-reporting companies to compete in the global market against companies that are not required to perform costly due diligence. In addition, an official from the Responsible Jewellery Council noted that gold is mined in many locations around the world

---

[49]According to Solutions for Hope officials, a tin smelter in the Katanga province is currently idle due to lack of consistent power, and another smelter in Rwanda, which is working toward certification by the Conflict-Free Smelter Program, has been idle for over 5 years.

and that production costs must always be taken into account. She stated that because the cost of due diligence for gold is usually proportional to risk, mining and sourcing responsibly in the Great Lakes Region could become more expensive than in other, lower-risk areas and that this represents a challenge to responsible sourcing efforts in the region.

Some Information about the Conflict Minerals Trade Is Publicly Available

Some stakeholders and governments in the region provide publicly available information related to in-region mining of conflict minerals and responsible sourcing initiatives. According to industry officials, the amount of publicly available data reported by responsible sourcing initiatives has increased over the past year. We found that iTSCi publishes various reports on its public website as part of its due diligence system for its members. These reports provide production and export data for tin, tantalum, and tungsten, including amounts traced through the iTSCi program, from three provinces in the DRC and Rwanda, as well as the mineral sales in U.S. dollars (for more details, including the applicable quantitative data, see app. IV). Also on its website, iTSCi publishes third-party audits of member companies, which assess the extent to which the companies have implemented the OECD Due Diligence Guidance and evaluate the companies' adherence to iTSCi's traceability and due diligence procedure. Additionally, iTSCi publishes governance assessments covering a range of topics. Examples include the security and political situation in areas without an iTSCi presence and the risks and performance, relative to the OECD Due Diligence Guidance and the SEC rule, of stakeholders that are part of, or play a role in monitoring, the conflict minerals supply chain.[50]

A comparison of production data from the conflict-free sourcing initiatives in the context of each country's or the region's total production or exports of tin, tantalum, tungsten, or gold is not feasible, because no reliable, comprehensive data on the production or export of conflict minerals for the countries or region are available. However, some quantitative government data on the production and exports of conflict minerals from the DRC and adjoining countries are available (see app. V). For example, the DRC government has published data on production and exports of all four conflict minerals and the Rwandan government has published export

---

[50]According to an iTSCi official, the governance assessments also include summaries of all incidents that have occurred and how they have been mitigated or otherwise resolved.

and value data for tin, tantalum, and tungsten. In addition, the International Trade Centre, a joint agency of the World Trade Organization and the UN, collects export data from governments that provide some context for the amount of conflict minerals declared as exported from the region, although these data do not identify minerals from conflict-free mines (see app. VI).

Some stakeholders indicated that the ICGLR may, at some point, be able to provide production and export data of conflict minerals from its member states, mostly Dodd-Frank-affected countries. This information could increase transparency at the individual country level. ICGLR requires its member states to implement a chain-of-custody tracking system for conflict minerals and to transmit data on mineral flows (i.e., quantities and destinations) at regular intervals to be incorporated in the ICGLR Regional Mineral Tracking Database. According to an ICGLR official, this database is populated with three types of information: (1) a historical record of mine sites in each country, (2) types and quantities of minerals produced at each mine site, and (3) mineral flows from the mine sites. According to ICGLR documentation, the data are used to track, analyze, and reconcile regional mineral flows and will become publicly available to ensure ICGLR's credibility. In November 2013, the ICGLR official stated that four of the 12 member countries had submitted information for the regional database: Rwanda, Uganda, the DRC, and, to a lesser extent, Burundi.

Little Additional Information on Rate of Sexual Violence in Eastern DRC and Adjoining Countries since July 2013

Since we reported in July 2013, no new population-based surveys related to sexual violence in the DRC, Uganda, Rwanda, or Burundi have been published. However, population-based surveys are underway, or being planned, in three of those countries—the DRC, Burundi, and Rwanda. In addition, some new case file data on sexual violence are available for all four countries. However, as we reported in 2011, case file data on sexual violence are not suitable for estimating a rate of sexual violence.

Several Population-Based Surveys Are Underway or Planned

Although no new surveys related to sexual violence in the DRC, Uganda, Rwanda, or Burundi have been published since July 2013, population-based surveys in the DRC, Burundi, and Rwanda are underway or planned by ICF International.[51] According to ICF International, data collection for a Demographic and Health Survey (DHS), which is a type of population-based survey, for the DRC is complete, but data resulting from the survey are not expected until September 2014 or later. ICF International also said that fieldwork for a DHS in Rwanda is likely to start in September or October 2014. ICF International indicated that a DHS is planned to start in Burundi in 2014; however, data collection may be delayed by funding gaps and, as a result, the survey may not take place until 2015.

Figure 4 shows the anticipated timelines for the population-based surveys on sexual violence that are currently underway or planned in the DRC, Burundi, and Rwanda. It also shows the publication dates for eight population-based surveys that provided data on the rate of sexual violence in eastern DRC, Rwanda, and Uganda that have been published since we started reporting on sexual violence in the region in 2011.

---

[51]ICF International implements the Demographic and Health Surveys (DHS) Program, which has provided technical assistance to more than 300 surveys in over 90 countries. The DHS Program provides capacity building to host-country implementing agencies through all survey stages, including survey design and sampling, training, field work, data tabulation and analysis, report writing, and dissemination and use of findings.

Figure 4: Timeline of Population-Based Surveys Estimating the Rate of Sexual Violence in Eastern DRC, Rwanda, Uganda, and Burundi

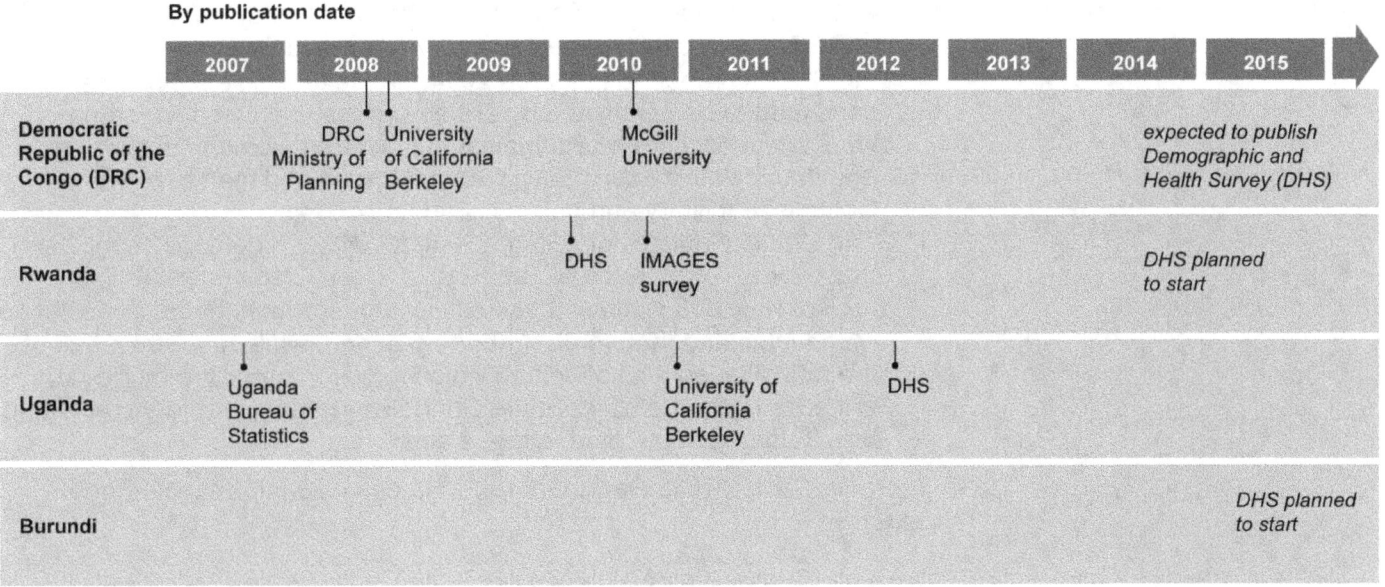

Source: GAO analysis. | GAO-14-575

Some Additional Case File Data on Sexual Violence Have Become Available since GAO's 2013 Report

Since 2013, some U.S. and UN agencies as well as researchers and an NGO have provided additional case file data on instances of sexual violence in the DRC and adjoining countries. In February 2014, State submitted its annual country reports on human rights practices to Congress, which provided the following data pertaining to sexual violence in the DRC, Burundi, and Uganda.[52] For example,

- In the DRC, the government reported 18,729 cases of sexual violence in 2012.
- In Burundi, 3,781 cases of gender-based violence were reported in 2010, according to a report compiled from family development centers throughout the country.
- In Uganda, 530 cases of rape were registered in 2012, and 301 of the alleged rapists were tried and convicted.

[52]U.S. Department of State, Bureau of Democracy, Human Rights and Labor, *Country Reports on Human Rights Practices for 2013*, accessed May 18, 2014, http://www.state.gov/j/drl/rls/hrrpt/humanrightsreport/index.htm#wrapper.

In addition, some UN entities reported case file information. For example:

- MONUSCO reported that between October 1, 2013, and December 5, 2013, it recorded acts of sexual violence against at least 79 women and 28 girls in conflict-affected provinces in the DRC.[53]
- MONUSCO reported in March 2014 that sexual violence crimes continued to be committed by armed groups and that such crimes were allegedly committed against at least four women, 35 girls, and one man by elements of illegal armed forces and members of the Congolese military and police in January 2014.
- The United Nations Joint Human Rights Office reported in April 2014 that between the period of January 2010 and December 2013, it registered 3,635 victims of sexual violence throughout the DRC.[54] The report indicated that, for the reporting period, while more than half of the total alleged acts of sexual violence were committee by illegal armed groups, members of the Congolese national military committed less than half of the other alleged acts.

Moreover, the DRC government reported case file information. For example:

- A report published in June 2013 by the DRC Ministry of Gender, the Family, and Child, with support by the UN Population Fund, highlighted cases of sexual violence in seven provinces in the country: Bandundu, Bas Congo, Katanga, Kinshasa, North Kivu, Orientale, and South Kivu.[55] Data in the report indicate that 10,322 incidents of sexual and gender-based violence were reported for the seven provinces in 2011 and that the number increased to 15,654 incidents in 2012. While the data also indicate that most of these assaults were committed by people dressed in civilian clothes—85 percent in 2011 and 78 percent in 2012—incidents involving armed groups between 2011 and 2012 increased in South Kivu from 36 to 76 percent, respectively, and in North Kivu from 32 to 61 percent, respectively.

---

[53]UN Security Council, *Report of the Secretary-General on the United Nations Organization Stabilization Mission in the Democratic Republic of the Congo*, S/2013/757 (New York, NY: Dec 17, 2013).

[54]*Progress and Obstacles in the Fight Against Impunity for Sexual Violence in the Democratic Republic of the Congo*, United Nations Joint Human Rights Office, April 2014.

[55]*Extent of Sexual Violence in the DRC and Actions to Fight against the Phenomenon of 2011 to 2012*, DRC Ministry of Gender, the Family, and Child; Kinshasa, June 2013. This report was not publicly available before we issued our report in July 2013.

An NGO also published case file information. For example:

- Médecins sans Frontières reported in March 2014 that in 2012 it provided medical care to a total of 4,037 women, men, and children after incidents of sexual violence in different project locations in the DRC.[56] It reported treating, in a 5-week period in late 2012 through early 2013, 95 of those individuals in one camp for Internally Displaced People in North Kivu.

Several factors make case file data unsuitable for estimating rates of sexual violence. First, because case file data are not aggregated across various sources, and because the extent to which various reports overlap is unclear, it is difficult to obtain complete data, or a sense of magnitude, from case files. Second, in case file data as well as surveys, time frames, locales, and definitions of sexual violence may be inconsistent across data collection operations. Third, case file data are not based on a random sample and the results of analyzing these data are not generalizable.

Conclusions

The long-running humanitarian crisis in eastern DRC, one of the most volatile areas in Africa, continues to be a concern for the U.S. government and the international community. As we have previously reported, section 1502 of the Dodd-Frank Wall Street Reform and Consumer Protection Act, enacted in 2010, is part of the U.S. effort to address the perpetration of sexual violence and mass killings in the DRC by armed groups who profit from the exploitation and trading of conflict minerals. We have compiled stakeholder data on the production and trade of conflict minerals that demonstrates, to some extent, the degree of transparency related to the conflict minerals trade. The actions undertaken by U.S. agencies in response to the Act could facilitate SEC-reporting companies' compliance with the SEC rule, promulgated pursuant to the Act, as they conduct due diligence and prepare the required annual reports disclosing the use and the origin of conflict minerals in their products. However, because Commerce has not met the Act's requirement that it compile by January 2013 a list of smelters and refiners—considered the "choke point" of the conflict minerals supply chain—these companies lack a source of critical information about the conflict minerals supply chain.

---

[56]Medecins sans Frontieres, *Everyday Emergency: Silent Suffering in the Democratic Republic of Congo*, Amsterdam, 2014.

Some stakeholders indicated that a comprehensive list of conflict minerals smelters and refiners could enable companies that are subject to the SEC rule to maintain transparency of the supply chain, and also provide companies the information they need for their SEC-required conflict minerals disclosure reports. Commerce cited several challenges that have hindered its providing the required list to Congress. However, having an action plan with associated timeframes could better position Commerce to report on the status of its efforts to produce a final list and provide it to Congress and to hold its personnel accountable for completing related activities.

Recommendation for Executive Action

To give Congress a sense of Commerce's efforts to produce a listing of all known conflict minerals processing facilities worldwide, as required by section 1502 of the Dodd-Frank Wall Street Reform and Consumer Protection Act, we recommend that the Secretary of Commerce provide to Congress a plan that outlines the steps, with associated timeframes, to develop and report the required information about smelters and refiners of conflict minerals worldwide.

Agency and Third Party Comments and Our Evaluation

We provided a draft of this report to SEC, State, USAID, and Commerce for their review. Commerce provided written comments, which we have reproduced in appendix VII. SEC and State provided technical comments, which we incorporated as appropriate. We also provided relevant portions of the draft report to some industry associations and other stakeholders of conflict minerals initiatives from whom we had obtained information during our review; some of these stakeholders provided technical comments that we incorporated as appropriate.

In its written comments, Commerce noted in response to our recommendation that it had provided and briefed us on a detailed outreach action plan that set forth how it intended to assemble the list of conflict minerals processing facilities required by the Act. However, as we have noted in this report, the document that Commerce provided was an outreach plan, consisting of a list of stakeholders that Commerce intended to contact to obtain information on conflict minerals smelters and refiners. The plan did not indicate a timeframe for completing and submitting to Congress the required listing of conflict minerals processing facilities worldwide. Commerce concurred with our recommendation and noted that it will submit a listing of all known conflict minerals processing facilities worldwide to Congress by September 1, 2014.

We are sending copies of this report to appropriate congressional committees. The report is also available at no charge on the GAO website at http://www.gao.gov/.

If you or your staffs have any questions about this report, please contact me at (202) 512-8612 or gianopoulosk@gao.gov. Contact points for our Offices of Congressional relations and Public Affairs may be found on the last page of this report. GAO staff who made key contributions to this report are listed in appendix VIII.

Kimberly M. Gianopoulos
Acting Director, International Affairs and Trade

List of Addressees

The Honorable Barbara Mikulski
Chairwoman
The Honorable Richard Shelby
Vice Chairman
Committee on Appropriations
United States Senate

The Honorable Tim Johnson
Chairman
The Honorable Mike Crapo
Ranking Member
Committee on Banking, Housing, and Urban Affairs
United States Senate

The Honorable Ron Wyden
Chairman
The Honorable Orrin G. Hatch
Ranking Member
Committee on Finance
United States Senate

The Honorable Robert Menendez
Chairman
The Honorable Bob Corker
Ranking Member
Committee on Foreign Relations
United States Senate

The Honorable Hal Rogers
Chairman
The Honorable Nita Lowey
Ranking Member
Committee on Appropriations
House of Representatives

The Honorable Jeb Hensarling
Chairman
The Honorable Maxine Waters
Ranking Member
Committee on Financial Services
House of Representatives

The Honorable Ed Royce
Chairman
The Honorable Eliot Engel
Ranking Member
Committee on Foreign Affairs
House of Representatives

The Honorable Dave Camp
Chairman
The Honorable Sander Levin
Ranking Member
Committee on Ways and Means
House of Representatives

Appendix I: Objectives, Scope, and Methodology

To determine the extent, if any, to which relevant U.S. agencies have engaged in activities related to responsible sourcing of conflict minerals, we interviewed officials who are cognizant of conflict minerals issues from the Departments of Commerce and State (State) and the United States Agency for International Development (USAID), and the Securities and Exchange Commission (SEC). We reviewed Section 1502 of the Dodd-Frank Wall Street Reform and Consumer Protection Act (Pub. L. No. 111-203) to identify the requirements for Commerce, State, SEC, and USAID related to implementation of section 1502. We also reviewed and analyzed reports and other documents from the agencies, such as the U.S. Strategy to Address the Linkages Between Human Rights Abuses, Armed Groups, Mining of Conflict Minerals, and Commercial Products; the conflict minerals rule; and maps of mineral-rich zones and areas under control of armed groups in the DRC. In addition, we reviewed and analyzed press releases, statements, plans, and guidance pertaining to conflict minerals and responsible sourcing that were issued by U.S. agencies. We also reviewed notes and agendas of responsible sourcing forums and other meetings attended by U.S. officials.

To analyze what is known about the status of, and any information provided by, initiatives focused on responsible sourcing of conflict minerals from the DRC and adjoining countries, we interviewed officials and reviewed and analyzed documents from State, USAID, and the United Nations Group of Experts on the Democratic Republic of the Congo (UNGoE); interviewed representatives and reviewed and analyzed guidance documents, reports, and presentations from foreign government, industry associations, multilateral organizations, companies, and nongovernmental organizations (NGOs). We selected these stakeholders based on their expertise on responsible sourcing issues, because they represented a range of perspectives on conflict minerals, and because we had established contacts with these entities on our last review.[1] In addition, some of the stakeholders we talked to have been working on the ground in the DRC. The stakeholders we spoke with constitute a nongeneralizable sample, and the information we gathered from them cannot be used to infer views of other stakeholders cognizant of conflict minerals issues. To determine which initiatives had expanded and which were new initiatives in the region, we interviewed U.S. agency

---

[1]GAO, *SEC Conflict Minerals Rule: Information on Responsible Sourcing and Companies Affected*, GAO-13-689 (Washington, D.C.: July 18, 2013).

officials and relevant stakeholders and reviewed documentation from
initiatives in the region. This report covers initiatives on which we have
previously reported and new initiatives since our 2013 report, as
described by stakeholders we interviewed.[2] However, it is possible that
the agency officials and stakeholders with whom we spoke may be
unaware of other stakeholders and/or responsible sourcing initiatives
active in the DRC and region. To determine the starting dates of the
initiatives, we interviewed stakeholders and reviewed the websites of the
various initiatives. To demonstrate what information stakeholders have
reported regarding responsible sourcing initiatives, we reviewed and
analyzed information published on the websites associated with the
various responsible sourcing initiatives. When reporting on information
provided by the initiatives and stakeholders, we are referring to
information such as reports published, amount of minerals mined per
region/country, amount of minerals exported, and value of minerals
produced and exported, including data covering 2012 through 2014. The
information gathered cannot be generalized and cannot be used to infer
views of other stakeholders cognizant of conflict minerals issues.

To demonstrate other sources of publicly available data on conflict
minerals, we collected and analyzed stakeholder and government data
covering 2003 through 2014. Because the data were not used to support
findings, conclusions, or recommendations, we did not assess their
reliability. To demonstrate the output of one of the in-region initiatives, we
collected production and export data for the ITRI Supply Chain Initiative
(iTSCi). We reviewed the production reports for three provinces in the
DRC and for Rwanda published on iTSCi's website, abbreviated the data
to include those most relevant to this study, and converted the data to
tons and thousands of U.S. dollars. A limitation of the data is that the
disaggregated production data–by mineral and mine–are proprietary to
iSTCi members, so it is not possible to quantify the total amount of any of
the minerals separately. We also collected conflict mineral production and
export data from the websites of the governments of the DRC and
Rwanda and from the International Trade Centre. We are presenting
these data in the appendixes of the report because these are the only
publicly available data we found for sourcing conflict minerals from the
region. There is no distinction in these data between minerals that are

---

[2]GAO, *Conflict Minerals Disclosure Rule: SEC's Actions and Stakeholder-Developed
Initiatives*, GAO-12-763 (Washington, D.C.: July 16, 2012) and GAO-13-689.

conflict-free and those that have supported armed groups. Moreover, none of these data can be generalized or be used to infer the total production or export of conflict minerals from the DRC and the adjoining countries.

In response to a mandate in the Dodd-Frank Wall Street Reform and Consumer Protection Act that GAO submit an annual report that assesses the rate of sexual violence in war-torn areas of the DRC and adjoining countries, we identified and assessed any additional published information available on sexual violence in war-torn eastern DRC, as well as three adjoining countries that border the DRC—Rwanda, Uganda, and Burundi—since our 2013 report on sexual violence in these areas.[3] During the course of our review, we interviewed officials from State and USAID and interviewed NGO representatives and researchers to discuss the collection of sexual violence-related data—including population-based surveys and case file data—in the DRC and adjoining countries. Specifically, we followed up with researchers and representatives from those groups we interviewed for our prior review on sexual violence rates in eastern DRC and adjoining countries, including a representative from the Human Rights Center at the University of California, Berkeley, School of Law and others officials. The team also traveled to New York City to meet with officials from the United Nations Population Fund, United Nations High Commissioner for Refugees, and the United Nations Special Representative of the Secretary-General on Sexual Violence in Conflict. We also conducted Internet literature searches to identify new academic articles containing any additional information on sexual violence since our 2013 report.[4]

We conducted this performance audit from September 2013 to June 2014 in accordance with generally accepted government auditing standards. Those standards require that we plan and perform the audit to obtain sufficient, appropriate evidence to provide a reasonable basis for our findings and conclusions based on our audit objectives. We believe that the evidence obtained provides a reasonable basis for our findings and conclusions based on our audit objectives.

---

[3]GAO-13-689. We did not include in our current report information from preliminary studies or reports.

[4]GAO-13-689.

Appendix II: State Department Map of Armed Groups Present at Mine Sites in the Democratic Republic of the Congo

Figure 5 depicts the most recent map published by the Department of State. The map focuses on the exploitation of tin, tantalum, tungsten, and gold in the provinces of North and South Kivu and parts of Orientale, Maniema, and Katanga provinces.

Appendix II: State Department Map of Armed
Groups Present at Mine Sites in the
Democratic Republic of the Congo

Figure 5: State Department Map of the Presence of Armed Groups at Mine Sites in the Democratic Republic of the Congo, as of February 2014

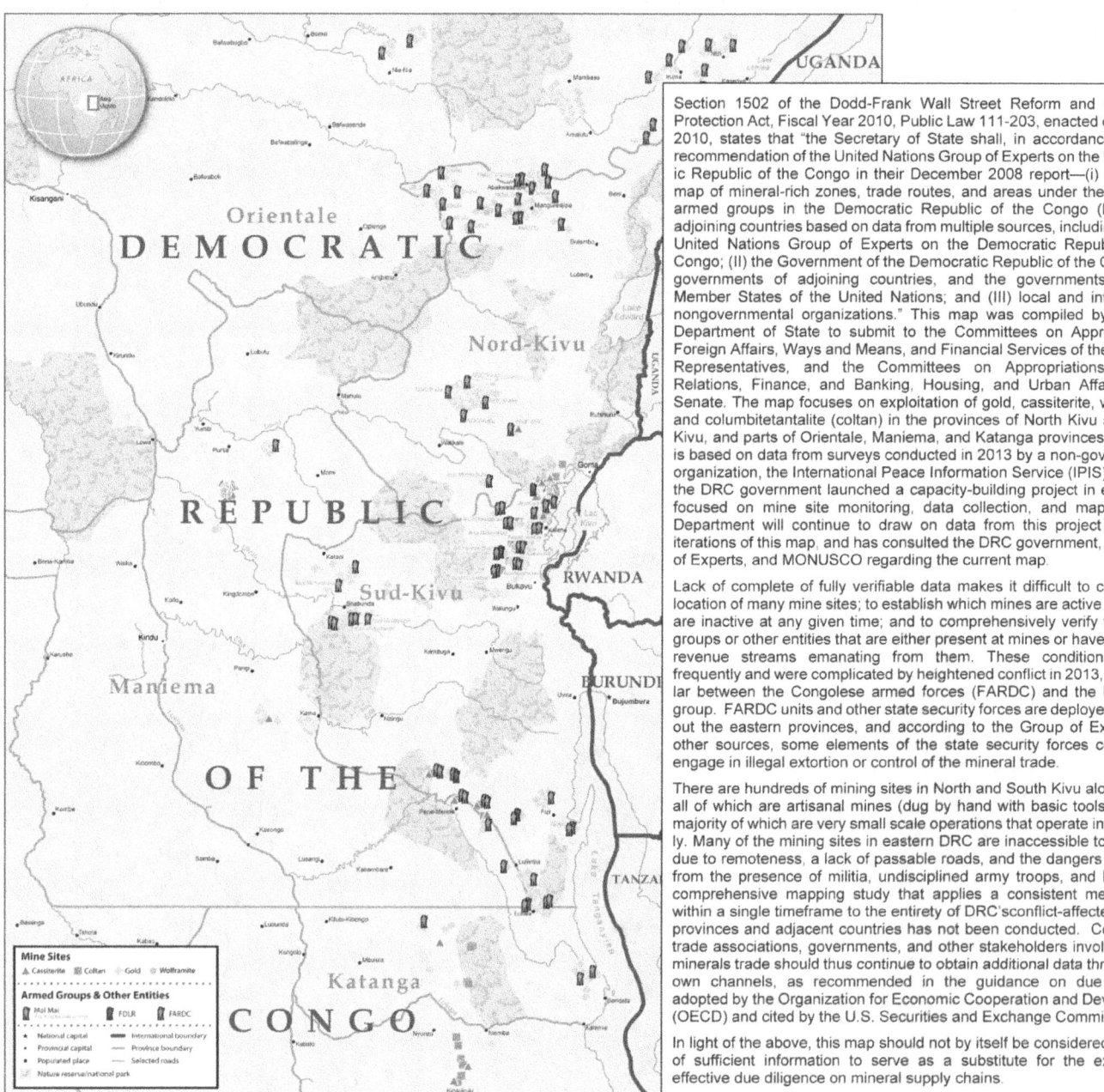

Section 1502 of the Dodd-Frank Wall Street Reform and Consumer Protection Act, Fiscal Year 2010, Public Law 111-203, enacted on July 21, 2010, states that "the Secretary of State shall, in accordance with the recommendation of the United Nations Group of Experts on the Democratic Republic of the Congo in their December 2008 report—(i) produce a map of mineral-rich zones, trade routes, and areas under the control of armed groups in the Democratic Republic of the Congo (DRC) and adjoining countries based on data from multiple sources, including—(I) the United Nations Group of Experts on the Democratic Republic of the Congo; (II) the Government of the Democratic Republic of the Congo, the governments of adjoining countries, and the governments of other Member States of the United Nations; and (III) local and international nongovernmental organizations." This map was compiled by the U.S. Department of State to submit to the Committees on Appropriations, Foreign Affairs, Ways and Means, and Financial Services of the House of Representatives, and the Committees on Appropriations, Foreign Relations, Finance, and Banking, Housing, and Urban Affairs of the Senate. The map focuses on exploitation of gold, cassiterite, wolframite, and columbitetantalite (coltan) in the provinces of North Kivu and South Kivu, and parts of Orientale, Maniema, and Katanga provinces. The map is based on data from surveys conducted in 2013 by a non-governmental organization, the International Peace Information Service (IPIS). IPIS and the DRC government launched a capacity-building project in early 2013 focused on mine site monitoring, data collection, and mapping. The Department will continue to draw on data from this project for future iterations of this map, and has consulted the DRC government, the Group of Experts, and MONUSCO regarding the current map.

Lack of complete of fully verifiable data makes it difficult to confirm the location of many mine sites; to establish which mines are active and which are inactive at any given time; and to comprehensively verify the armed groups or other entities that are either present at mines or have access to revenue streams emanating from them. These conditions change frequently and were complicated by heightened conflict in 2013, in particular between the Congolese armed forces (FARDC) and the M23 rebel group. FARDC units and other state security forces are deployed throughout the eastern provinces, and according to the Group of Experts and other sources, some elements of the state security forces continue to engage in illegal extortion or control of the mineral trade.

There are hundreds of mining sites in North and South Kivu alone, nearly all of which are artisanal mines (dug by hand with basic tools), and the majority of which are very small scale operations that operate intermittently. Many of the mining sites in eastern DRC are inaccessible to outsiders due to remoteness, a lack of passable roads, and the dangers stemming from the presence of militia, undisciplined army troops, and bandits. A comprehensive mapping study that applies a consistent methodology within a single timeframe to the entirety of DRC'sconflict-affected eastern provinces and adjacent countries has not been conducted. Companies, trade associations, governments, and other stakeholders involved in the minerals trade should thus continue to obtain additional data through their own channels, as recommended in the guidance on due diligence adopted by the Organization for Economic Cooperation and Development (OECD) and cited by the U.S. Securities and Exchange Commission.

In light of the above, this map should not by itself be considered a source of sufficient information to serve as a substitute for the exercise of effective due diligence on mineral supply chains.

Source: State. | GAO-14-575

Appendix III: SEC Flowchart Summary of the Disclosure Process for the Final Conflict Minerals Rule

When the SEC adopted the conflict minerals rule in August 2012, it published a flowchart summary of the final rule to guide SEC-reporting companies affected by the rule through the disclosure process (see fig 6). In general, the process reflects that an SEC-reporting company needs to (1) determine whether its manufactured products contain conflict minerals, (2) determine whether conflict minerals are necessary to the functionality or production of the product and if it originated in the DRC or an adjoining country, and (3) possibly conduct due diligence and potentially provide a Conflict Minerals Report.

Appendix III: SEC Flowchart Summary of the
Disclosure Process for the Final Conflict
Minerals Rule

Figure 6: SEC Flowchart Summary of Conflict Minerals Rule

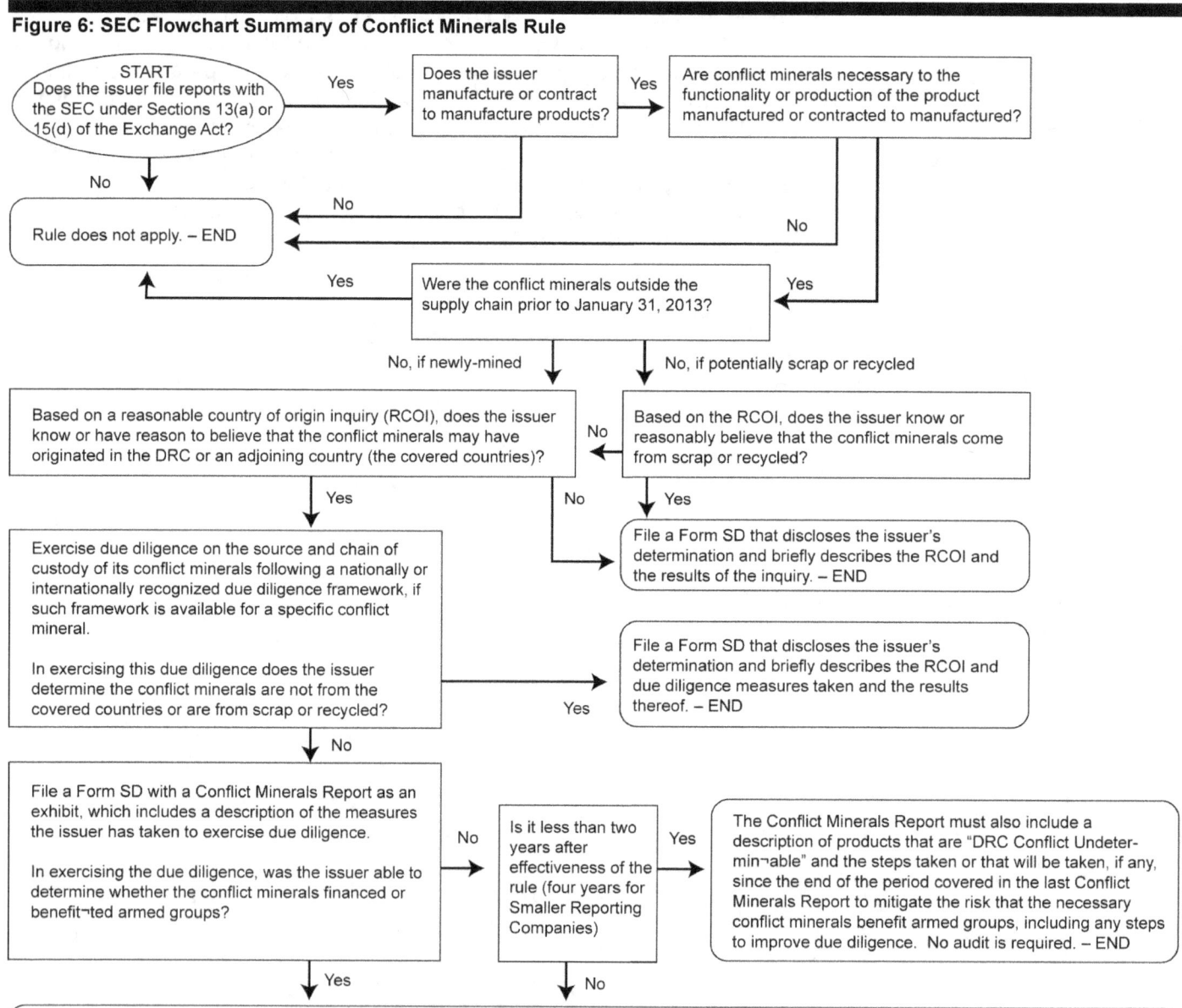

Appendix III: SEC Flowchart Summary of the
Disclosure Process for the Final Conflict
Minerals Rule

Note: SEC indicated that the flowchart is intended to be used as a guide and that issuers should refer to the text in the rule for a more comprehensive description of the rule's requirements. Further, SEC indicated that, as a result of the appeals court decision, SEC's stay order, and SEC staff's guidance, some of the steps outlined in the flowchart have been modified pending further action by SEC or a court.

Appendix IV: Sample Data from the ITRI Supply Chain Initiative

The ITRI Supply Chain Initiative (iTSCi) publishes qualitative and quantitative information on its projects in the DRC and Rwanda on its website. The information includes production data for minerals that have been mined and traded employing the iTSCi traceability system, audits of iTSCi member companies, and assessments of the political and security situation in various sites in the DRC and Rwanda. The mineral production and export data include minerals mined under the auspices of other stakeholder-led initiatives in the region. Almost all of the initiatives employ the iTSCi traceability system to track the mining and trading of minerals along the supply chain.[1]

One limitation of the data is that the production data–disaggregated by mineral and mine–are proprietary to iSTCi members. Therefore, it is not possible to quantify the total quantity or value of any of the minerals separately.[2]

Tables 2-7 provide iTSCi production in metric tons and mineral sales in thousands of U.S. dollars for tin, tungsten, and tantalum coming from several provinces in the DRC, including Maniema, South Kivu, and Katanga.

Table 2: Production of Minerals from Maniema Covered by iTSCi for Q1 and Q2 of 2013, in Metric Tons

2013	Tin	Tin/Tantalum[a]	Tin/Tungsten[a]	Tantalum/Tungsten[a]	Tungsten
Q1	17		11		1
Q2	225	1	17	1	
Total	242	1	28	1	1

Source: GAO based on iTSCi data. | GAO-14-575

Note: Empty cells indicate no recorded production.

[a]iTSCi data include traced material that are reported as combinations of more than one mineral.

---

[1]Because the data were not used to support findings, conclusions, or recommendations, we did not assess their reliability.

[2]Detailed data showing production and exports of each of the conflict minerals are proprietary to iTSCi members.

Table 3: Sales of Minerals from Maniema Covered by iTSCi for Q1 and Q2 of 2013, in Thousands of U.S. Dollars

2013	Tin	Tin/Tantalum[a]	Tin/Tungsten[a]	Tantalum/Tungsten[a]	Tungsten
Q1	$87		$46		$1
Q2	$1,163	$5	$84	$3	
Total	$1,250	$5	$130	$3	$1

Source: GAO based on iTSCi data. | GAO-14-575

Note: Empty cells indicate no recorded sales.

[a]iTSCi data include traced material that are reported as combinations of more than one mineral.

Table 4: Production of Minerals from South Kivu Covered by iTSCi for Q4 of 2012 through Q2 of 2013, in Metric Tons

Year/Quarter	Tin	Tin/Tantalum[a]
2012/Q4	181	
2013/Q1	200	
2013/Q2	80	1
Total	460	1

Source: GAO based on iTSCi data. | GAO-14-575

Note: Empty cells indicate no recorded production. Totals may not add due to rounding.

[a]iTSCi data include traced material that are reported as combinations of more than one mineral.

Table 5: Sales of Minerals from South Kivu Covered by iTSCi for Q4 of 2012 through Q2 of 2013, in Thousands of U.S. Dollars

Year/Quarter	Tin	Tin/Tantalum[a]
2012/Q4	$760	
2013/Q1	$800	
2013/Q2	$286	$3
Total	$1,847	$3

Source: GAO based on iTSCi data. | GAO-14-575

Note: Empty cells indicate no recorded sales. Totals may not add due to rounding.

[a]iTSCi data include traced material that are reported as combinations of more than one mineral.

GAO-14-575 Conflict Minerals

Table 6: Production of Minerals from Katanga Covered by iTSCi for Q2 of 2011 through Q2 of 2013, in Metric Tons

Year/Quarter	Tin	Tin/Tantalum[a]	Tin/Tungsten[a]	Tantalum	Tantalum/Tungsten[a]	Tungsten
2011/Q2	796	193	2	54		3
2011/Q3	1,436	234	2	51		16
2011/Q4	779	121	2	128		26
2012/Q1	753	252	15	114		12
2012/Q2	651	275	40	60	2	15
2012/Q3	671	258	18	64	2	40
2012/Q4	497	188	7	45		29
2013/Q1	340	211	7	34		9
2013/Q2	648	441	2	40	0.4	6
Total	**6,572**	**2,172**	**97**	**588**	**3**	**155**

Source: GAO based on iTSCi data. | GAO-14-575

Note: Empty cells indicate no recorded production. Totals may not add due to rounding.

[a]iTSCi data include traced material that are reported as combinations of more than one mineral.

Table 7: Sales of Minerals from Katanga Covered by iTSCi for Q2 of 2011 through Q2 of 2013, in Thousands of U.S. Dollars

Year/Quarter	Tin	Tin/Tantalum[a]	Tin/Tungsten[a]	Tantalum	Tantalum/Tungsten[a]	Tungsten
2011/Q2	$5,166	$1,290	$14	$1,548		$21
2011/Q3	$9,839	$1,746	$18	$1,733		$122
2011/Q4	$4,072	$718	$40	$4,448		$152
2012/Q1	$4,224	$1,783	$67	$3,758		$70
2012/Q2	$3,701	$1,811	$193	$2,012	$7	$97
2012/Q3	$3,352	$1,720	$172	$2,114	$5	$181
2012/Q4	$2,906	$1,268	$106	$1,571		$105
2013/Q1	$2,112	$1,449	$38	$1,092		$74
2013/Q2	$3,744	$3,583	$11	$1,502	$2	$19
Total	**$39,117**	**$15,367**	**$659**	**$19,778**	**$15**	**$840**

Source: GAO based on iTSCi data. | GAO-14-575

Note: Empty cells indicate no recorded sales. Totals may not add due to rounding.

[a]iTSCi data include traced material that are reported as combinations of more than one mineral.

Tables 8 and 9 provide iTSCi production in tons and mineral sales in thousands of U.S. dollars for tin, tungsten and tantalum in Rwanda.

Table 8: Production of Minerals from Rwanda Covered by iTSCi for Q2 of 2011 through Q2 of 2013, in Metric Tons

Year/Quarter	Tin	Tin/Tantalum[a]	Tin/Tungsten[a]	Tin/Tantalum/Tungsten[a]	Tantalum	Tantalum/Tungsten[a]	Tungsten
2011/Q2	1,393	442	3	3	56	1	353
2011/Q3	1,318	406	1	4	56		438
2011/Q4	1,387	381	14	1	41		528
2012/Q1	825	316	8	3	102	3	575
2012/Q2	671	397	5	16	108	1	605
2012/Q3	780	509	4	26	162	1	582
2012/Q4	842	489	2	24	165	2	454
2013/Q1	915	678	1	3	178		538
2013/Q2	827	799	1		248		486
Total	8,958	4,417	39	79	1,115	8	4,560

Source: GAO based on iTSCi data. | GAO-14-575

Note: Empty cells indicate no recorded production. Totals may not add due to rounding.

[a]iTSCi data include traced material that are reported as combinations of more than one mineral.

Table 9: Sales of Minerals from Rwanda Covered by iTSCi for Q2 of 2011 through Q2 of 2013, in Thousands of U.S. Dollars

Year/Quarter	Tin	Tin/Tantalum[a]	Tin/Tungsten[a]	Tin/Tantalum/Tungsten[a]	Tantalum	Tantalum/Tungsten[a]	Tungsten
2011/Q2	$11,481	$6,217	$32	$25	$1,095	$8	$1,988
2011/Q3	$9,533	$4,778	$16	$26	$972		$2,935
2011/Q4	$9,333	$4,423	$154	$10	$720		$3,608
2012/Q1	$4,874	$4,383	$92	$26	$2,068	$17	$4,007
2012/Q2	$3,369	$4,980	$31	$98	$2,098	$15	$4,691
2012/Q3	$4,273	$6,394	$27	$176	$3,473	$12	$4,891
2012/Q4	$6,026	$8,008	$26	$263	$4,148	$35	$4,235
2013/Q1	$6,982	$11,031	$19	$59	$5,654		$6,678
2013/Q2	$5,988	$14,857	$24		$8,331		$4,605
Total	$61,859	$65,070	$421	$683	$28,560	$87	$37,637

Source: GAO based on iTSCi data. | GAO-14-575

Note: Empty cells indicate no recorded sales. Totals may not add due to rounding.

[a]iTSCi data include traced material that are reported as combinations of more than one mineral.

Appendix V: Conflict Mineral Production and Export Data as Reported by the DRC and Rwandan Governments

The DRC Ministry of Mines published data on the volume of production and exports for tin, tantalum, tungsten, and gold for 2003-2012 (see tables 10-13).[1]

Table 10: Total Volume of Tin Production and Export from DRC for 2003-2012, in Metric Tons

	Production	Export
2003	2,986	2,986
2004	2,317	2,945
2005	5,171	5,971
2006	5,528	2,388
2007	16,050	14,694
2008	20,013	19,189
2009	16,584	15,512
2010	11,943	13,415
2011	8,921	9,267
2012	7,189	8,018
Total	**96,702**	**94,385**

Source: GAO based on DRC Ministry of Mines. | GAO-14-575

---

[1]The DRC Ministry of Mines statistics also include production and export data for other minerals. Because the data were not used to support findings, conclusions, or recommendations, we did not assess their reliability.

Table 11: Total Volume of Tantalum Production and Export from DRC for 2003-2012, in Metric Tons

	Production	Export
2003	47	47
2004	78	32
2005	184	185
2006	31	24
2007	393	393
2008	530	531
2009	509	464
2010	492	440
2011	2,199	536
2012	574	586
Total	**5,037**	**3,238**

Source: GAO based on DRC Ministry of Mines. | GAO-14-575

Table 12: Total Volume of Tungsten Production and Export from DRC for 2003-2012, in Metric Tons

	Production	Export
2003	No data	100
2004	272	190
2005	405	311
2006	1,001	471
2007	1,265	1,194
2008	621	725
2009	458	365
2010	44	45
2011	84	87
2012	197	71
Total	**4,347**	**3,559**

Source: GAO based on DRC Ministry of Mines. | GAO-14-575

Table 13: Total Volume of Gold Production and Export from DRC for 2003-2012, in Metric Tons

	Production	Export
2003	No data	No data
2004	0.7	0.0
2005	0.6	0.6
2006	0.3	0.1
2007	0.1	0.1
2008	0.1	0.1
2009	0.2	0.2
2010	0.2	0.2
2011	0.3	0.2
2012	2.8	2.4
Total	**5.3**	**3.9**

Source: GAO based on DRC Ministry of Mines. | GAO-14-575

The Rwanda Natural Resources Authority published data on the volume and value of tin, tantalum and tungsten exported from Rwanda from January to August of 2013 (see tables 14 and 15).[2]

Table 14: Total Volume of Tin, Tantalum, and Tungsten Exports from Rwanda January-August 2013, in Metric Tons

	Tin	Tantalum	Tungsten
January	421	84	184
February	224	48	130
March	475	284	185
April	510	251	230
May	458	273	157
June	267	212	177
July	396	288	151
August	407	245	164
Total	**3,158**	**1,686**	**1,378**

Source: GAO based on Rwanda Natural Resources Authority. | GAO-14-575

Note: Totals may not add due to rounding.

---

[2]Because the data were not used to support findings, conclusions, or recommendations, we did not assess their reliability.

Table 15: Total Value of Tin, Tantalum, and Tungsten Exports from Rwanda January-August 2013, in Thousands of U.S. Dollars

	Tin	Tantalum	Tungsten
January	$5,386	$4,953	$2,178
February	$2,803	$3,012	$1,564
March	$8,314	$16,379	$2,118
April	$6,352	$15,736	$3,915
May	$5,365	$16,583	$2,075
June	$3,206	$12,373	$2,559
July	$4,297	$17,822	$2,103
August	$4,509	$15,144	$2,277
Total	**$40,233**	**$102,002**	**$18,789**

Source: GAO based on Rwanda Natural Resources Authority. | GAO-14-575

Note: Totals may not add due to rounding.

Appendix VI: Conflict Minerals Data from the International Trade Centre Data on Global Conflict Mineral Imports

The International Trade Centre (ITC), a joint agency of the World Trade Organization and the United Nations (UN) compiles a Trade Map with data including the global exports in tons and export value of tin, tantalum, tungsten and gold from the DRC and adjoining countries, as available for fiscal years 2009-2013 (see tables 16-31 for ITC data as of June 2014).[1] The ITC calculated these data using the UN Commodity Trade Statistics Database, which compiles trade data from UN member countries.

These data do not provide a comprehensive depiction of the flow of conflict minerals exported from the DRC and adjoining countries; rather, they are an estimate based on imports data from reporting partner countries. Furthermore, these data may include imports of conflict minerals that have financed armed groups.[2]

In many instances, there are no data listed for a particular mineral or year. There were no data for import volume or value of conflict minerals in the ITC database for the Republic of the Congo (Congo-Brazzaville) or South Sudan.

Table 16: ITC Estimates of Exports of Conflict Minerals from the Democratic Republic of the Congo for Fiscal Years 2009-2013, in Metric Tons

	Tin	Tantalum[b]	Tungsten	Gold
FY2009	160[a]	121[a]	471[a]	No quantity[a]
FY2010	2,589[a]	252[a]	87[a]	0 [a]
FY2011	510[a]	101[a]	10[a]	0 [a]
FY2012	1,670[a]	326[a]		0 [a]
FY2013	2,621[a]	329[a]	95[a]	0 [a]
Total	**7,550**	**1,129**	**663**	**0[a]**

Source: GAO analysis of Trade Map data. | GAO-14-575

Note: According to the ITC, if there is no record in the export dataset for a specific mineral and a specific partner country, they consider that the country has not exported the mineral for that year and publish a zero value. "No quantity" means that the country under review has reported a value but no quantity for the product and partner under review. Empty cells indicate that no partner country has reported importation of that mineral from that country.

[1]The Trade Map (or Market Access Map, Investment Map and Standards Map, respectively), International Trade Centre, www.intracen.org/marketanalysis.

[2]Because the data were not used to support findings, conclusions, or recommendations, we did not assess their reliability.

[a]According to the ITC, these estimates of exports have been reconstructed on the basis of data reported by importing partner countries, known as mirror statistics. The ITC states that mirror statistics are a "second-best solution" when no data exist but are subject to limitations, including the omission of non-reporting countries, particularly in Africa.

[b]Export data for tantalum ores and concentrates also include exports of niobium and vanadium ores and concentrates.

Table 17: ITC Estimates of Export Value of Conflict Minerals from the DRC for F Fiscal Years 2009-2013, in Thousands of U.S. Dollars

	Tin	Tantalum[b]	Tungsten	Gold
FY2009	$1,061[a]	$2,575[a]	$4,357[a]	$1,251[a]
FY2010	$23,045[a]	$5,161[a]	$806a	$1,140[a]
FY2011	$8,786[a]	$9,131[a]	$263[a]	$4,426[a]
FY2012	$17,719[a]	$24,006[a]		$1,394[a]
FY2013	$32,628[a]	$22,142[a]	$1,339[a]	$2,729[a]
Total	$83,239	$63,015	$6,765	$10,940

Source: GAO analysis of Trade Map data. | GAO-14-575

Note: According to the ITC, empty cells indicate that no partner country has reported importation of that mineral from that country.

[a]According to the ITC, these estimates of exports have been reconstructed on the basis of data reported by importing partner countries, known as mirror statistics. The ITC states that mirror statistics are a "second-best solution" when no data exist, but are subject to limitations, including the omission of non-reporting countries, particularly in Africa.

[b]Export data for tantalum ores and concentrates also include exports of niobium and vanadium ores and concentrates.

Table 18: ITC Estimates of Exports of Conflict Minerals from Angola for Fiscal Years 2009-2012, in Metric Tons

	Tin	Tantalum[b]	Tungsten	Gold
FY2009				
FY2010				
FY2011			No quantity[a]	0
FY2012		19[a]		
FY2013	No quantity[a]	28[a]		
Total		47		0

Source: GAO analysis of Trade Map data. | GAO-14-575

Note: According to the ITC, if there is no record in the export dataset for a specific mineral and a specific partner country, they consider that the country has not exported the mineral for that year and publish a zero value. "No quantity" means that the country under review has reported a value but no quantity for the product and partner under review. Empty cells indicate that no partner country has reported importation of that mineral from that country.

[a]According to the ITC, these estimates of exports have been reconstructed on the basis of data reported by importing partner countries, known as mirror statistics. The ITC states that mirror

statistics are a "second-best solution" when no data exist ,but are subject to limitations, including the omission of non-reporting countries, particularly in Africa.

[b]Export data for tantalum ores and concentrates also include exports of niobium and vanadium ores and concentrates.

Table 19: ITC Estimates of Export Value of Conflict Minerals from Angola for Fiscal Years 2009-2013, in Thousands of U.S. Dollars

	Tin	Tantalum[b]	Tungsten	Gold
FY2009				
FY2010				
FY2011			$0[a]	$90[a]
FY2012		$31[a]		
FY2013	$0[a]	$7		
Total	$0	$38	$0	$90

Source: GAO analysis of Trade Map data. | GAO-14-575

Note: According to the ITC, if there is no record in the export dataset for a specific mineral and a specific partner country, they consider that the country has not exported the mineral for that year and publish a zero value. Empty cells indicate that no partner country has reported importation of that mineral from that country.

[a]According to the ITC, these estimates of exports have been reconstructed on the basis of data reported by importing partner countries, known as mirror statistics. The ITC states that mirror statistics are a "second-best solution" when no data exist, but are subject to limitations, including the omission of non-reporting countries, particularly in Africa.

[b]Export data for tantalum ores and concentrates also include exports of niobium and vanadium ores and concentrates.

Table 20: ITC Estimates of Exports of Conflict Minerals from Burundi for Fiscal Years 2009-2012, in Metric Tons

	Tin	Tantalum[a]	Tungsten	Gold
FY2009	26	0	264	1
FY2010	32	0	503	0
FY2011	0	17	330	1
FY2012	0	0	32	2
FY2013	No quantity	76	148	3
Total	58	93	1,277	7

Source: GAO analysis of Trade Map data. | GAO-14-575

Note: According to the ITC, if there is no record in the export dataset for a specific mineral and a specific partner country, they consider that the country has not exported the mineral for that year and publish a zero value. "No quantity" means that the country under review has reported a value but no quantity for the product and partner under review.

[a]Export data for tantalum ores and concentrates also include exports of niobium and vanadium ores and concentrates.

Table 21: ITC Estimates of Export Value of Conflict Minerals from Burundi for Fiscal Years 2009-2013, in Thousands of U.S. Dollars

	Tin	Tantalum[a]	Tungsten	Gold
FY2009	$175	$0	$1,547	$28,979
FY2010	$297	$0	$2,951	$13,003
FY2011	$15	$20	$4,607	$59,047
FY2012	$0	$0	$226	$105,196
FY2013	$0	$2,753	$1,776	$121,470
Total	$487	$2,773	$11,107	$327,695

Source: GAO analysis of Trade Map data. | GAO-14-575

Note: According to the ITC, if there is no record in the export dataset for a specific mineral and a specific partner country, they consider that the country has not exported the mineral for that year and publish a zero value.

[a]Export data for tantalum ores and concentrates also include exports of niobium and vanadium ores and concentrates.

Table 22: ITC Estimates of Exports of Conflict Minerals from Central African Republic for Fiscal Years 2009-2012, in Metric Tons

	Tin	Tantalum[a]	Tungsten	Gold
FY2009				24
FY2010				49
FY2011				21
FY2012				6
FY2013				691
Total				791

Source: GAO analysis of Trade Map data. | GAO-14-575

Note: According to the ITC, empty cells indicate that no partner country has reported importation of that mineral from that country.

[a]Export data for tantalum ores and concentrates also include exports of niobium and vanadium ores and concentrates.

Table 23: ITC Estimates of Export Value of Conflict Minerals from Central African Republic for Fiscal Years 2009-2013, in Thousands of U.S. Dollars

	Tin	Tantalum[a]	Tungsten	Gold
FY2009				$473
FY2010				$1,277
FY2011				$2,509
FY2012				$1,367
FY2013				$318
Total				$5,944

Source: GAO analysis of Trade Map data. | GAO-14-575

Note: According to the ITC, empty cells indicate that no partner country has reported importation of that mineral from that country.

[a]Export data for tantalum ores and concentrates also include exports of niobium and vanadium ores and concentrates.

Table 24: ITC Estimates of Exports of Conflict Minerals from Rwanda for Fiscal Years 2009-2012, in Metric Tons

	Tin	Tantalum[a]	Tungsten	Gold
FY2009	5,224	958	945	0
FY2010	6,477	827	879	0
FY2011	7,314	915	784	0
FY2012	4,658	1,139	1,372	0
FY2013	4,820	2,466	2,119	0
Total	28,493	6,305	6,099	0

Source: GAO analysis of Trade Map data. | GAO-14-575

Note: According to the ITC, if there is no record in the export dataset for a specific mineral and a specific partner country, they consider that the country has not exported the mineral for that year and publish a zero value.

[a]Export data for tantalum ores and concentrates also include exports of niobium and vanadium ores and concentrates.

Table 25: ITC Estimates of Export Value of Conflict Minerals from Rwanda for Fiscal Years 2009-2013, in Thousands of U.S. Dollars

	Tin	Tantalum[a]	Tungsten	Gold
FY2009	$34,235	$18,082	$6,283	$856
FY2010	$65,834	$20,034	$7,254	$170
FY2011	$101,921	$39,000	$11,677	0
FY2012	$52,912	$56,698	$21,354	0
FY2013	$57,957	$134,575	$28,866	0
Total	**$312,859**	**$268,389**	**$75,434**	**$1,026**

Source: GAO analysis of Trade Map data. | GAO-14-575

Note: According to the ITC, if there is no record in the export dataset for a specific mineral and a specific partner country, they consider that the country has not exported the mineral for that year and publish a zero value.

[a]Export data for tantalum ores and concentrates also include exports of niobium and vanadium ores and concentrates.

Table 26: ITC Estimates of Export of Conflict Minerals from Tanzania for Fiscal Years 2009-2012, in Metric Tons

	Tin	Tantalum[a]	Tungsten	Gold
FY2009	0	0	0	402
FY2010	1	0	0	325
FY2011	66	160	0	43
FY2012	71	112	0	319
FY2013	57	No quantity	No quantity	140
Total	**195**	**272**	**0**	**1,229**

Source: GAO analysis of Trade Map data. | GAO-14-575

Note: According to the ITC, if there is no record in the export dataset for a specific mineral and a specific partner country, they consider that the country has not exported the mineral for that year and publish a zero value. "No quantity" means that the country under review has reported a value but no quantity for the product and partner under review.

[a]Export data for tantalum ores and concentrates also include exports of niobium and vanadium ores and concentrates.

Table 27: ITC Estimates of Export Value of Conflict Minerals from Tanzania for Fiscal Years 2009-2013, in Thousands of U.S. Dollars

	Tin	Tantalum[a]	Tungsten	Gold
FY2009	$0	$0	$0	$818,598
FY2010	$5	$0	$0	$966,077
FY2011	$373	$59	$0	$1,718,196
FY2012	$351	$153	$0	$1,863,327
FY2013	$329	$0	$0	$1,549,580
Total	**$1,058**	**$212**	**$0**	**$6,915,778**

Source: GAO analysis of Trade Map data. | GAO-14-575

Note: According to the ITC, if there is no record in the export dataset for a specific mineral and a specific partner country, they consider that the country has not exported the mineral for that year and publish a zero value.

[a]Export data for tantalum ores and concentrates also include exports of niobium and vanadium ores and concentrates.

Table 28: ITC Estimates of Exports of Conflict Minerals from Uganda for Fiscal Years 2009-2012, in Metric Tons

	Tin	Tantalum[a]	Tungsten	Gold
FY2009	7	No quantity	0	1
FY2010	No quantity	No quantity	0	1
FY2011	0	No quantity	No quantity	0
FY2012	No quantity	No Quantity	100	0
FY2013	12	8	91	0
Total	**19**	**8**	**191**	**2**

Source: GAO analysis of Trade Map data. | GAO-14-575

Note: According to the ITC, if there is no record in the export dataset for a specific mineral and a specific partner country, they consider that the country has not exported the mineral for that year and publish a zero value. "No quantity" means that the country under review has reported a value but no quantity for the product and partner under review.

[a]Export data for tantalum ores and concentrates also include exports of niobium and vanadium ores and concentrates.

Table 29: ITC Estimates of Export Value of Conflict Minerals from Uganda for Fiscal Years 2009-2013, in Thousands of U.S. Dollars

	Tin	Tantalum[a]	Tungsten	Gold
FY2009	$2	$0	$0	$13,100
FY2010	$0	$0	$0	$30,072
FY2011	$1	$0	$0	$6,795
FY2012	$0	$0	$979	$9,163
FY2013	$128	$22	$972	$3,128
Total	**$131**	**$22**	**$1,951**	**$62,258**

Source: GAO analysis of Trade Map data. | GAO-14-575

Note: According to the ITC, if there is no record in the export dataset for a specific mineral and a specific partner country, they consider that the country has not exported the mineral for that year and publish a zero value.

[a]Export data for tantalum ores and concentrates also include exports of niobium and vanadium ores and concentrates.

Table 30: ITC Estimates of Exports of Conflict Minerals from Zambia for Fiscal Years 2009-2012, in Metric Tons

	Tin	Tantalum[a]	Tungsten	Gold
FY2009	27	No quantity	0	695
FY2010	0	No quantity	23	555
FY2011	28	0	72	2
FY2012	0	No quantity	0	1,492
FY2013	6	0	0	4
Total	**61**	**0**	**95**	**2,748**

Source: GAO analysis of Trade Map data. | GAO-14-575

Note: According to the ITC, if there is no record in the export dataset for a specific mineral and a specific partner country, they consider that the country has not exported the mineral for that year and publish a zero value. "No quantity" means that the country under review has reported a value but no quantity for the product and partner under review.

[a]Export data for tantalum ores and concentrates also include exports of niobium and vanadium ores and concentrates.

Table 31: ITC Estimates of Export Value of Conflict Minerals from Zambia for Fiscal Years 2009-2013, in Thousands of U.S. Dollars

	Tin	Tantalum[a]	Tungsten	Gold
FY2009	$77	$0	$0	$19,004
FY2010	$1	$0	$12	$46,411
FY2011	$50	$0	$6	$81,040
FY2012	$0	$0	$0	$140,744
FY2013	$4	$0	$0	$164,079
Total	**$132**	**$0**	**$18**	**$451,278**

Source: GAO analysis of Trade Map data. | GAO-14-575

Note: According to the ITC, if there is no record in the export dataset for a specific mineral and a specific partner country, they consider that the country has not exported the mineral for that year and publish a zero value.

[a]Export data for tantalum ores and concentrates also include exports of niobium and vanadium ores and concentrates.

Appendix VII: Comments from the Department of Commerce

THE DEPUTY SECRETARY OF COMMERCE
Washington, D.C. 20230

June 13, 2014

Ms. Kimberley M. Gianopoulos
Acting Director, International Affairs and Trade
U.S. Government Accountability Office
441 G Street NW
Washington, DC 20548

Dear Ms. Gianopoulos:

Thank you for providing the Department of Commerce (Commerce) with a copy of the U.S. Government Accountability Office (GAO) proposed report entitled *Conflict Minerals: Stakeholder Options for Responsible Sourcing Expanding, but More Information on Smelters Is Needed* (GAO-14-575) for our review and comment prior to issuance of the report.

As we noted in our meetings with GAO staff both in January and May, the International Trade Administration (ITA) faced significant challenges in implementing Commerce's reporting requirements under Section 1502(d) of the Dodd-Frank Act. ITA is focused on a two-part mission: (1) advancing Commerce's statutory mandate to foster, promote, and develop the foreign commerce of the United States; (2) creating prosperity by strengthening the international competitiveness of U.S. industry, promoting trade and investment, and ensuring fair trade and compliance with trade laws and agreements.

As a result of the focus on its mission, at the time the Dodd-Frank Act was enacted, ITA did not have staff available or trained to carry out the conflict minerals reporting requirements specified therein. Instead, we were required to survey existing capabilities, divert resources from other initiatives, and train existing staff in order to implement those requirements. As we explained in our meetings with GAO staff, based on our meetings with the Department of the Interior's U.S. Geological Survey (USGS), we believe that USGS has ongoing program activities, existing resources, and institutional expertise and capacity that would have allowed it to more readily meet the Dodd-Frank Act requirement regarding reporting on a list of all known conflict mineral processing facilities.

Despite these obstacles, ITA staff has successfully completed its outreach plan and has collected information from a number of publicly available sources in order to develop the "listing of all known conflict mineral processing facilities worldwide," called for by the Dodd-Frank Act. We agree with GAO that developing a plan of action is the first step in developing such a list. In fact, on February 26, we provided a detailed action plan to GAO, setting forth exactly how ITA intends to assemble this list, and also briefed GAO on this action plan during our two meetings. Implications to the contrary in GAO's draft report are inaccurate.

Ms. Kimberley M. Gianopoulos
Page 2

With respect to GAO's recommendation that "the Secretary of Commerce provide to Congress a plan that outlines the steps, with associated timeframes, to develop and report the required information about smelters and refiners of conflict minerals worldwide," we plan to implement GAO's recommendation by submitting a listing of all known conflict mineral processing facilities worldwide to Congress by September 1.

Thank you again for the opportunity to provide review and comment on the draft report.

Sincerely,

Bruce Andrews
Acting Deputy Secretary of Commerce

Appendix VIII: GAO Contacts and Staff Acknowledgments

GAO Contact	Kimberly M. Gianopoulos, (202) 512-8612 or gianopoulosk@gao.gov
Staff Acknowledgments	In addition to the individual named above, Godwin Agbara (Assistant Director), Russ Burnett, Etana Finkler, Justin Fisher, Julia Jebo Grant, Ernie Jackson, Jill Lacey, Reid Lowe, Andrea Riba Miller, and John O'Trakoun made key contributions to this report.

GAO's Mission	The Government Accountability Office, the audit, evaluation, and investigative arm of Congress, exists to support Congress in meeting its constitutional responsibilities and to help improve the performance and accountability of the federal government for the American people. GAO examines the use of public funds; evaluates federal programs and policies; and provides analyses, recommendations, and other assistance to help Congress make informed oversight, policy, and funding decisions. GAO's commitment to good government is reflected in its core values of accountability, integrity, and reliability.
Obtaining Copies of GAO Reports and Testimony	The fastest and easiest way to obtain copies of GAO documents at no cost is through GAO's website (http://www.gao.gov). Each weekday afternoon, GAO posts on its website newly released reports, testimony, and correspondence. To have GAO e-mail you a list of newly posted products, go to http://www.gao.gov and select "E-mail Updates."
Order by Phone	The price of each GAO publication reflects GAO's actual cost of production and distribution and depends on the number of pages in the publication and whether the publication is printed in color or black and white. Pricing and ordering information is posted on GAO's website, http://www.gao.gov/ordering.htm. Place orders by calling (202) 512-6000, toll free (866) 801-7077, or TDD (202) 512-2537. Orders may be paid for using American Express, Discover Card, MasterCard, Visa, check, or money order. Call for additional information.
Connect with GAO	Connect with GAO on Facebook, Flickr, Twitter, and YouTube. Subscribe to our RSS Feeds or E-mail Updates. Listen to our Podcasts. Visit GAO on the web at www.gao.gov.
To Report Fraud, Waste, and Abuse in Federal Programs	Contact: Website: http://www.gao.gov/fraudnet/fraudnet.htm E-mail: fraudnet@gao.gov Automated answering system: (800) 424-5454 or (202) 512-7470
Congressional Relations	Katherine Siggerud, Managing Director, siggerudk@gao.gov, (202) 512-4400, U.S. Government Accountability Office, 441 G Street NW, Room 7125, Washington, DC 20548
Public Affairs	Chuck Young, Managing Director, youngc1@gao.gov, (202) 512-4800 U.S. Government Accountability Office, 441 G Street NW, Room 7149 Washington, DC 20548